THE GOSPEL
TO ST.

Translated from the Latin Vulgate
Diligently Compared with the Hebrew, Greek,
and Other Editions in Divers Languages

THE NEW TESTAMENT
First Published by the English College at Rheims
A.D. 1582

With Annotations

The Whole Revised and Diligently Compared with
the Latin Vulgate by Bishop Richard Challoner
A.D. 1749-1752

1

The Gospel According to St. John
The Whole Revised and Diligently Compared with
the Latin Vulgate by Bishop Richard Challoner
A.D. 1749-1752

Fonck, Leopold. "St. John the Evangelist." The Catholic Encyclopedia. Vol. 8. New York: Robert Appleton Company, 1910.

The Gospel According to St. John, which is included in the New Testament, was first published by the English College at Rheims in 1582.

The New Testament was revised and diligently compared with the Latin Vulgate by Bishop Richard Challoner from 1749-1752

CONTENTS

ST. JOHN THE EVANGELIST

I. New Testament Accounts

John was the son of Zebedee and Salome, and the brother of James the Greater. In the Gospels the two brothers are often called after their father "the sons of Zebedee" and received from Christ the honourable title of Boanerges, i.e. "sons of thunder" (Mark 3:17). Originally they were fishermen and fished with their father in the Lake of Genesareth. According to the usual and entirely probable explanation they became, however, for a time disciples of John the Baptist, and were called by Christ from the circle of John's followers, together with Peter and Andrew, to become His disciples (John 1:35-42). The first disciples returned with their new Master from the Jordan to Galilee and apparently both John and the others remained for some time with Jesus (cf. John ii, 12, 22; iv, 2, 8, 27 sqq.). Yet after the second return from Judea, John and his companions went back again to their trade of fishing until he and they were called by Christ to definitive discipleship (Matthew 4:18-22; Mark 1:16-20). In the lists of the Apostles John has the second place (Acts 1:13), the third (Mark 3:17), and the fourth (Matthew 10:3; Luke 6:14), yet always after James with the exception of a few passages (Luke 8:51; 9:28 in the Greek text; Acts 1:13).

From James being thus placed first, the conclusion is drawn that John was the younger of the two brothers. In any case John had a prominent position in the Apostolic body. Peter, James, and he were the only witnesses of the raising of Jairus's daughter (Mark 5:37), of the Transfiguration (Matthew 17:1), and of the Agony in Gethsemani (Matthew 26:37). Only he and Peter were sent into the city to make the preparation for the Last Supper (Luke 22:8). At the Supper itself his place was next to Christ on Whose breast he leaned (John 13:23, 25). According to the general interpretation John was also that "other disciple" who with Peter followed Christ after the arrest into the palace of the high-priest (John 18:15). John alone remained near his beloved Master at the foot of the Cross on Calvary with the Mother of Jesus and the pious women, and took the desolate Mother into his care as the last legacy of Christ (John 19:25-27). After the Resurrection John with Peter was the first of the disciples to hasten to the grave and he was the first to believe that Christ had truly risen (John 20:2-10). When later Christ appeared at the Lake of Genesareth John was also the first of the seven disciples present who recognized his Master standing on the shore (John 21:7). The Fourth Evangelist has shown us most clearly how close the relationship was in which he always stood to his Lord and Master by the title with which he is accustomed to indicate

6

himself without giving his name: "the disciple whom Jesus loved". After Christ's Ascension and the Descent of the Holy Spirit, John took, together with Peter, a prominent part in the founding and guidance of the Church. We see him in the company of Peter at the healing of the lame man in the Temple (Acts 3:1 sqq.). With Peter he is also thrown into prison (Acts 4:3). Again, we find him with the prince of the Apostles visiting the newly converted in Samaria (Acts 8:14).

We have no positive information concerning the duration of this activity in Palestine. Apparently John in common with the other Apostles remained some twelve years in this first field of labour, until the persecution of Herod Agrippa I led to the scattering of the Apostles through the various provinces of the Roman Empire (cf. Acts 12:1-17). Notwithstanding the opinion to the contrary of many writers, it does not appear improbable that John then went for the first time to Asia Minor and exercised his Apostolic office in various provinces there. In any case a Christian community was already in existence at Ephesus before Paul's first labours there (cf. "the brethren", Acts 18:27, in addition to Priscilla and Aquila), and it is easy to connect a sojourn of John in these provinces with the fact that the Holy Ghost did not permit the Apostle Paul on his second missionary journey to proclaim the Gospel in Asia, Mysia, and Bithynia (Acts 16:6 sq.). There is just as little against such an acceptation in the later account in Acts of St. Paul's third missionary journey. But in any case such a sojourn by John in Asia in this first period was neither long nor uninterrupted. He returned with the other disciples to Jerusalem for the Apostolic Council (about A.D. 51). St. Paul in opposing his enemies in Galatia names John explicitly along with Peter and James the Less as a "pillar of the Church", and refers to the recognition which his Apostolic preaching of a Gospel free from the law received from these three, the most prominent men of the old Mother-Church at Jerusalem (Galatians 2:9). When Paul came again to Jerusalem after the second and after the third journey (Acts 18:22; 21:17 sq.) he seems no longer to have met John there. Some wish to draw the conclusion from this that John left Palestine between the years 52 and 55.

Of the other New-Testament writings, it is only from the three Epistles of John and the Apocalypse that anything further is learned concerning the person of the Apostle. We may be permitted here to take as proven the unity of the author of these three writings handed down under the name of John and his identity with the Evangelist. Both the Epistles and the Apocalypse, however, presuppose that their author John belonged to the multitude of personal eyewitnesses of the life and work of Christ (cf. especially 1 John 1:1-5; 4:14), that he had lived for a long time in Asia Minor, was thoroughly acquainted with the conditions existing in the various Christian communities there, and that he had a position of authority recognized by all Christian communities as leader of this part of the Church. Moreover, the Apocalypse tells us that its author was on the island of Patmos "for the word of God and for the testimony of

Jesus", when he was honoured with the heavenly Revelation contained in the Apocalypse (Revelation 1:9).

II. The Alleged Presbyter John

The author of the Second and Third Epistles of John designates himself in the superscription of each by the name (ho presbyteros), "the ancient", "the old". Papias, Bishop of Hierapolis, also uses the same name to designate the "Presbyter John" as in addition to Aristion, his particular authority, directly after he has named the presbyters Andrew, Peter, Philip, Thomas, James, John, and Matthew (in Eusebius, Church History III.39.4). Eusebius was the first to draw, on account of these words of Papias, the distinction between a Presbyter John and the Apostle John, and this distinction was also spread in Western Europe by St. Jerome on the authority of Eusebius. The opinion of Eusebius has been frequently revived by modern writers, chiefly to support the denial of the Apostolic origin of the Fourth Gospel. The distinction, however, has no historical basis. First, the testimony of Eusebius in this matter is not worthy of belief. He contradicts himself, as in his "Chronicle" he expressly calls the Apostle John the teacher of Papias ("ad annum Abrah 2114"), as does Jerome also in Ep. lxxv, "Ad Theodoram", iii, and in Illustrious Men 18. Eusebius was also influenced by his erroneous doctrinal opinions as he denied the Apostolic origin of the Apocalypse and ascribed this writing to an author differing from St. John but of the same name. St. Irenæus also positively designates the Apostle and Evangelist John as the teacher of Papias, and neither he nor any other writer before Eusebius had any idea of a second John in Asia (Against Heresies V.33.4). In what Papias himself says the connection plainly shows that in this passage by the word presbyters only Apostles can be understood. If John is mentioned twice the explanation lies in the peculiar relationship in which Papias stood to this, his most eminent teacher. By inquiring of others he had learned some things indirectly from John, just as he had from the other Apostles referred to. In addition he had received information concerning the teachings and acts of Jesus directly, without the intervention of others, from the still living "Presbyter John", as he also had from Aristion. Thus the teaching of Papias casts absolutely no doubt upon what the New-Testament writings presuppose and expressly mention concerning the residence of the Evangelist John in Asia.

III. The Later Accounts of John

The Christian writers of the second and third centuries testify to us as a tradition universally recognized and doubted by no one that the Apostle and Evangelist John lived in Asia Minor in the last decades of the first century and from Ephesus had guided the Churches of that province. In his "Dialogue with Tryphon" (Chapter 81) St. Justin Martyr refers to "John, one of the Apostles of Christ" as a witness who had lived

10

"with us", that is, at Ephesus. St. Irenæus speaks in very many places of the Apostle John and his residence in Asia and expressly declares that he wrote his Gospel at Ephesus (Against Heresies III.1.1), and that he had lived there until the reign of Trajan (loc. cit., II, xxii, 5). With Eusebius (Church History III.13.1) and others we are obliged to place the Apostle's banishment to Patmos in the reign of the Emperor Domitian (81-96). Previous to this, according to Tertullian's testimony (De praescript., xxxvi), John had been thrown into a cauldron of boiling oil before the Porta Latina at Rome without suffering injury. After Domitian's death the Apostle returned to Ephesus during the reign of Trajan, and at Ephesus he died about A.D. 100 at a great age. Tradition reports many beautiful traits of the last years of his life: that he refused to remain under the same roof with Cerinthus (Irenaeus "Ad. haer.", III, iii, 4); his touching anxiety about a youth who had become a robber (Clemens Alex., "Quis dives salvetur", xiii); his constantly repeated words of exhortation at the end of his life, "Little children, love one another" (Jerome, "Comm. in ep. ad. Gal.", vi, 10). On the other hand the stories told in the apocryphal Acts of John, which appeared as early as the second century, are unhistorical invention.

IV. Feasts of St. John

St. John is commemorated on 27 December, which he originally shared with St. James the Greater.

At Rome the feast was reserved to St. John alone at an early date, though both names are found in the Carthage Calendar, the Hieronymian Martyrology, and the Gallican liturgical books. The "departure" or "assumption" of the Apostle is noted in the Menology of Constantinople and the Calendar of Naples (26 September), which seems to have been regarded as the date of his death. The feast of St. John before the Latin Gate, supposed to commemorate the dedication of the church near the Porta Latina, is first mentioned in the Sacramentary of Adrian I (772-95).

V. St. John in Christian Art

Early Christian art usually represents St. John with an eagle, symbolizing the heights to which he rises in the first chapter of his Gospel. The chalice as symbolic of St. John, which, according to some authorities, was not adopted until the thirteenth century, is sometimes interpreted with reference to the Last Supper, again as connected with the legend according to which St. John was handed a cup of poisoned wine, from which, at his blessing, the poison rose in the shape of a serpent. Perhaps the most natural explanation is to be found in the words of Christ to John and James "My chalice indeed you shall drink" (Matthew 20:23).

THE HOLY GOSPEL OF JESUS CHRIST ACCORDING TO ST. JOHN

St. John the Apostle and Evangelist was the son of Zebedee and Salome, brother to James the Greater. He was called the Beloved disciple of Christ and stood by at his Crucifixion. He wrote the Gospel after the other Evangelists, about sixty-three years after our Lord's Ascension. Many things that they had omitted were supplied by him. The original was written in Greek; and by the Greeks he is titled: The Divine, St. Jerome relates that, when he was earnestly requested by the brethren to write the Gospel, he answered he would do it, if by ordering a common fast, they would all put up their prayers together to the Almighty God; which being ended replenished with the clearest and fullest revelation coming from Heaven, he burst forth into that preface: IN THE BEGINNING WAS THE WORD.

JOHN CHAPTER 1

The divinity and incarnation of Christ. John bears
witness of him. He begins to call his disciples.

1 In the beginning was the Word: and the Word was
with God: and the Word was God. 2 The same was in
the beginning with God. 3 All things were made by
him: and without him was made nothing that was
made. 4 In him was life: and the life was the light of
men. 5 And the light shineth in darkness: and the
darkness did not comprehend it. 6 There was a man
sent from God, whose name was John. 7 This man
came for a witness, to give testimony of the light, that
all men might believe through him. 8 He was not the
light, but was to give testimony of the light. 9 That
was the true light, which enlighteneth every man that
cometh into this world. 10 He was in the world: and
the world was made by him: and the world knew him
not. 11 He came unto his own: and his own received
him not. 12 But as many as received him, he gave
them power to be made the sons of God, to them that
believe in his name. 13 Who are born, not of blood,
nor of the will of the flesh, nor of the will of man, but
of God. 14 And the Word was made flesh and dwelt
among us (and we saw his glory, the glory as it were
of the only begotten of the Father), full of grace and
truth. 15 John beareth witness of him and crieth out,
saying: This was he of whom I spoke: He that shall
come after me is preferred before me: because he was
before me. 16 And of his fulness we all have received:

and grace for grace. 17 For the law was given by Moses: grace and truth came by Jesus Christ. 18 No man hath seen God at any time: the only begotten Son who is in the Bosom of the Father, he hath declared him. 19 And this is the testimony of John, when the Jews sent from Jerusalem priests and Levites to him, to ask him: Who art thou? 20 And he confessed and did not deny: and he confessed: I am not the Christ. 21 And they asked him: What then? Art thou Elias? And he said: I am not. Art thou the prophet? And he answered: No. 22 They said therefore unto him: Who art thou, that we may give an answer to them that sent us? What sayest thou of thyself? 23 He said: I am the voice of one crying in the wilderness, make straight the way of the Lord, as said the prophet Isaias. 24 And they that were sent were of the Pharisees. 25 And they asked him and said to him: Why then dost thou baptize, if thou be not Christ, nor Elias, nor the prophet? 26 John answered them, saying: I baptize with water: but there hath stood one in the midst of you, whom you know not. 27 The same is he that shall come after me, who is preferred before me: the latchet of whose shoe I am not worthy to loose. 28 These things were done in Bethania, beyond the Jordan, where John was baptizing. 29 The next day, John saw Jesus coming to him; and he saith: Behold the Lamb of God. Behold him who taketh away the sin of the world. 30 This is he of whom I said: After me there cometh a man, who is preferred before me: because he was before me. 31 And I knew him not: but that he may be made manifest in Israel, therefore am I come baptizing with water. 32 And John gave testimony, saying: I saw the Spirit coming down, as a dove from heaven; and he remained upon him. 33 And I knew him not: but he who sent me to baptize with water said to me: He upon whom thou shalt see the Spirit descending and remaining upon him, he it is that baptizeth with the Holy Ghost. 34 And I saw: and I gave testimony that this is the Son of God. 35 The next day again John stood and two of his disciples. 36 And beholding Jesus walking, he saith: Behold the Lamb of God. 37 And the two disciples heard him speak: and they followed Jesus. 38 And Jesus turning and seeing them following him, saith to them: What seek you? Who said to him: Rabbi (which is to say, being interpreted, Master), where dwellest thou? 39 He saith to them: Come and see. They came and saw where he abode: and they stayed with him that day. Now it was about the tenth hour. 40 And Andrew, the brother of Simon Peter, was one of the two who had heard of John and followed him. 41 He findeth first his brother Simon and saith to him: We have found the Messias, which is, being interpreted, the Christ. 42 And he brought him to Jesus. And Jesus looking upon him, said: Thou art Simon the son of Jona. Thou shalt be called Cephas, which is interpreted Peter. 43 On the following day, he would go forth into Galilee: and he findeth Philip, And Jesus saith to him: follow me. 44 Now Philip was of Bethsaida, the city of Andrew and Peter. 45 Philip findeth Nathanael and saith to him: We have found him of whom Moses, in the law and the prophets did write, Jesus the son of Joseph of

Nazareth. 46. And Nathanael said to him: Can any thing of good come from Nazareth? Philip saith to him: Come and see. 47 Jesus saw Nathanael coming to him and he saith of him: Behold an Israelite indeed, in whom there is no guile. 48 Nathanael saith to him: Whence knowest thou me? Jesus answered and said to him: Before that Philip called thee, when thou wast under the fig tree, I saw thee. 49 Nathanael answered him and said: Rabbi: Thou art the Son of God. Thou art the King of Israel. 50 Jesus answered and said to him: Because I said unto thee, I saw thee under the fig tree, thou believest: greater things than these shalt thou see. 51 And he saith to him: Amen, amen, I say to you, you shall see the heaven opened and the angels of God ascending and descending upon the Son of man.

JOHN CHAPTER 2

Christ changes water into wine. He casts the sellers out of the temple.

1 And the third day, there was a marriage in Cana of Galilee: and the mother of Jesus was there. 2 And Jesus also was invited, and his disciples, to the marriage. 3 And the wine failing, the mother of Jesus saith to him: They have no wine. 4 And Jesus saith to her: Woman, what is that to me and to thee? My hour is not yet come.[1] 5 His mother saith to the waiters:

---

1 What is that to me, etc... These words of our Saviour,

Whatsoever he shall say to you, do ye. 6 Now there were set there six waterpots of stone, according to the manner of the purifying of the Jews, containing two or three measures apiece. 7 Jesus saith to them: Fill the waterpots with water. And they filled them up to the brim. 8 And Jesus saith to them: Draw out now and carry to the chief steward of the feast. And they carried it. 9 And when the chief steward had tasted the water made wine and knew not whence it was, but the waiters knew who had drawn the water: the chief steward calleth the bridegroom, 10 And saith to him: Every man at first setteth forth good wine, and when men have well drunk, then that which is worse. But thou hast kept the good wine until now. 11 This beginning of miracles did Jesus in Cana of Galilee and manifested his glory. And his disciples believed in him. 12 After this, he went down to Capharnaum, he and his mother and his brethren and his disciples: and they remained there not many days. 13 And the pasch

---

spoken to his mother, have been understood by some commentators as harsh, they not considering the next following verse: Whatsoever he shall say to you, do ye, which plainly shows that his mother knew of the miracle that he was to perform, and that it was at her request he wrought it; besides the manner of speaking the words as to the tone, and the countenance shown at the same time, which could only be known to those who were present, or from what had followed: for words indicating anger in one tone of voice, would be understood quite the reverse in another.

of the Jews was at hand: and Jesus went up to Jerusalem. 14 And he found in the temple them that sold oxen and sheep and doves, and the changers of money sitting. 15 And when he had made, as it were, a scourge of little cords, he drove them all out of the temple, the sheep also and the oxen: and the money of the changers he poured out, and the tables he overthrew. 16 And to them that sold doves he said: Take these things hence, and make not the house of my Father a house of traffic. 17 And his disciples remembered, that it was written: The zeal of thy house hath eaten me up. 18 The Jews, therefore, answered, and said to him: What sign dost thou shew unto us, seeing thou dost these things? 19 Jesus answered and said to them: Destroy this temple; and in three days I will raise it up. 20 The Jews then said: Six and forty years was this temple in building; and wilt thou raise it up in three days? 21 But he spoke of the temple of his body. 22 When therefore he was risen again from the dead, his disciples remembered that he had said this: and they believed the scripture and the word that Jesus had said. 23 Now when he was at Jerusalem, at the pasch, upon the festival day,many believed in his name, seeing his signs which he did. 24 But Jesus did not trust himself unto them: for that he knew all men, 25 And because he needed not that any should give testimony of man: for he knew what was in man.

JOHN CHAPTER 3

Christ's discourse with Nicodemus. John's testimony.

1 And there was a man of the Pharisees, named Nicodemus, a ruler of the Jews. 2 This man came to Jesus by night and said to him: Rabbi, we know that thou art come a teacher from God; for no man can do these signs which thou dost, unless God be with him. 3 Jesus answered and said to him: Amen, amen, I say to thee, unless a man be born again, he cannot see the kingdom of God. 4 Nicodemus saith to him: How can a man be born when he is old? Can he enter a second time into his mother's womb and be born again? 5 Jesus answered: Amen, amen, I say to thee, unless a man be born again of water and the Holy Ghost, he cannot enter into the kingdom of God.[2] 6 That which is born of the flesh is flesh: and that which is born of the Spirit is spirit. 7 Wonder not that I said to thee: You must be born again. 8 The Spirit breatheth where he will and thou hearest his voice: but thou knowest not whence he cometh and whither he goeth. So is every one that is born of the Spirit. 9 Nicodemus answered and said to him: How can these things be done? 10 Jesus answered and said to him: Art thou a master in Israel, and knowest not these things? 11 Amen, amen, I say to thee that we speak what we know and we

---

2 Unless a man be born again, etc... By these words our Saviour hath declared the necessity of baptism; and by the word water it is evident that the application of it is necessary with the words. Matt. 28. 19.

testify what we have seen: and you receive not our testimony. 12 If I have spoken to you earthly things, and you believe not: how will you believe, if I shall speak to you heavenly things? 13 And no man hath ascended into heaven, but he that descended from heaven, the Son of man who is in heaven. 14 And as Moses lifted up the serpent in the desert, so must the Son of man be lifted up: 15 That whosoever believeth in him may not perish, but may have life everlasting. 16 For God so loved the world, as to give his only begotten Son: that whosoever believeth in him may not perish, but may have life everlasting. 17 For God sent not his Son into the world, to judge the world: but that the world may be saved by him. 18 He that believeth in him is not judged. But he that doth not believe is already judged: because he believeth not in the name of the only begotten Son of God.[3] 19 And this is the judgment: Because the light is come into the world and men loved darkness rather than the light: for their works were evil.[4] 20 For every one that doth evil hateth the light and cometh not to the light, that his works may not be reproved. 21 But he that doth truth cometh to the light, that his works may be made

---

3 Is not judged... He that believeth, viz., by a faith working through charity, is not judged, that is, is not condemned; but the obstinate unbeliever is judged, that is, condemned already, by retrenching himself from the society of Christ and his church.

4 The judgment... That is, the cause of his condemnation.

manifest: because they are done in God.[5] 22 After these things, Jesus and his disciples came into the land of Judea: and there he abode with them and baptized. 23 And John also was baptizing in Ennon near Salim: because there was much water there. And they came and were baptized. 24 For John was not yet cast into prison. 25 And there arose a question between some of John's disciples and the Jews, concerning purification. 26 And they came to John and said to him: Rabbi, he that was with thee beyond the Jordan, to whom thou gavest testimony: behold, he baptizeth and all men come to him. 27 John answered and said: A man cannot receive any thing, unless it be given him from heaven. 28 You yourselves do bear me witness that I said that I am not Christ, but that I am sent before him. 29 He that hath the bride is the bridegroom: but the friend of the bridegroom, who standeth and heareth Him, rejoiceth with joy because of the bridegroom's voice. This my joy therefore is fulfilled. 30 He must increase: but I must decrease. 31 He that cometh from above is above all. He that is of the earth, of the earth he is, and of the earth he speaketh. He that cometh from heaven is above all. 32 And what he hath seen and heard, that he testifieth: and no man receiveth his testimony. 33 He that hath received his testimony hath set to his seal that God is true. 34 For he whom God hath sent speaketh the words of God: for God doth not

---

5 He that doth truth... that is, he that acteth according to truth, which here signifies the Law of God. Thy law is truth. Psa. 118. 142.

give the Spirit by measure. 35 The Father loveth the Son: and he hath given all things into his hand. 36 He that believeth in the Son hath life everlasting: but he that believeth not the Son shall not see life: but the wrath of God abideth on him.

JOHN CHAPTER 4

Christ talks with the Samaritan woman.
He heals the ruler's son.

1 When Jesus therefore understood the Pharisees had heard that Jesus maketh more disciples and baptizeth more than John, 2 (Though Jesus himself did not baptize, but his disciples), 3 He left Judea and went again into Galilee. 4 And he was of necessity to pass through Samaria. 5 He cometh therefore to a city of Samaria, which is called Sichar, near the land which Jacob gave to his son Joseph. 6 Now Jacob's well was there. Jesus therefore, being wearied with his journey, sat thus on the well. It was about the sixth hour. 7 There cometh a woman of Samaria, to draw water. Jesus saith to her: Give me to drink. 8 For his disciples were gone into the city to buy meats. 9 Then that Samaritan woman saith to him: How dost thou, being a Jew; ask of me to drink, who am a Samaritan woman? For the Jews do not communicate with the Samaritans. 10 Jesus answered and said to her: If thou didst know the gift of God and who he is that saith to thee: Give me to drink; thou perhaps wouldst have

asked of him, and he would have given thee living water. 11 The woman saith to him: Sir, thou hast nothing wherein to draw, and the well is deep. From whence then hast thou living water? 12 Art thou greater than our father Jacob, who gave us the well and drank thereof, himself and his children and his cattle? 13 Jesus answered and said to her: Whosoever drinketh of this water shall thirst again: but he that shall drink of the water that I will give him shall not thirst for ever. 14 But the water that I will give him shall become in him a fountain of water, springing up into life everlasting. 15 The woman said to him: Sir, give me this water, that I may not thirst, nor come hither to draw. 16 Jesus saith to her: Go, call thy husband, and come hither. 17 The woman answered and said: I have no husband. Jesus said to her: Thou hast said well: I have no husband. 18 For thou hast had five husbands: and he whom thou now hast is not thy husband. This, thou hast said truly. 19 The woman saith to him: Sir, I perceive that thou art a prophet. 20 Our fathers adored on this mountain: and you say that at Jerusalem is the place where men must adore.[6] 21 Jesus saith to her: Woman, believe me that the hour cometh, when you shall neither on this mountain, nor in Jerusalem, adore the Father. 22 You adore that which you know not: we adore that which we know. For salvation is of the Jews. 23 But the hour cometh and now is, when the true adorers shall adore the

---

6 This mountain... Garizim, where the Samaritans had their schismatical temple.

Father in spirit and in truth. For the Father also seeketh such to adore him. 24 God is a spirit: and they that adore him must adore him in spirit and in truth. 25 The woman saith to him: I know that the Messias cometh (who is called Christ): therefore, when he is come, he will tell us all things. 26 Jesus saith to her: I am he, who am speaking with thee. 27 And immediately his disciples came. And they wondered that he talked with the woman. Yet no man said: What seekest thou? Or: Why talkest thou with her? 28 The woman therefore left her waterpot and went her way into the city and saith to the men there: 29 Come, and see a man who has told me all things whatsoever I have done. Is not he the Christ? 30 They went therefore out of the city and came unto him. 31 In the mean time, the disciples prayed him, saying: Rabbi, eat. 32 But he said to them: I have meat to eat which you know not. 33 The disciples therefore said one to another: Hath any man brought him to eat? 34 Jesus saith to them: My meat is to do the will of him that sent me, that I may perfect his work. 35 Do not you say: There are yet four months, and then the harvest cometh? Behold, I say to you, lift up your eyes, and see the countries. For they are white already to harvest. 36 And he that reapeth receiveth wages and gathereth fruit unto life everlasting: that both he that soweth and he that reapeth may rejoice together. 37 For in this is the saying true: That it is one man that soweth, and it is another that reapeth. 38 I have sent you to reap that in which you did not labour. Others have laboured: and you have entered into their labours. 39 Now of that city many of the Samaritans believed in him, for the word of the woman giving testimony: He told me all things whatsoever I have done. 40 So when the Samaritans were come to him, they desired that he would tarry there. And he abode there two days. 41 And many more believed in him, because of his own word. 42 And they said to the woman: We now believe, not for thy saying: for we ourselves have heard him and know that this is indeed the Saviour of the world. 43 Now after two days, he departed thence and went into Galilee. 44 For Jesus himself gave testimony that a prophet hath no honour in his own country. 45 And when he was come into Galilee, the Galileans received him, having seen all the things he had done at Jerusalem on the festival day: for they also went to the festival day. 46 He came again therefore into Cana of Galilee, where he made the water wine. And there was a certain ruler, whose son was sick at Capharnaum. 47 He having heard that Jesus was come from Judea into Galilee, sent to him and prayed him to come down and heal his son: for he was at the point of death. 48 Jesus therefore said to him: Unless you see signs and wonders, you believe not. 49 The ruler saith to him: Lord, come down before that my son die. 50 Jesus saith to him: Go thy way. Thy son liveth. The man believed the word which Jesus said to him and went his way. 51 And as he was going down, his servants met him: and they brought word, saying, that his son lived. 52 He asked therefore of them the hour wherein he grew better. And they said to him: Yesterday at the seventh hour, the fever left him. 53

The father therefore knew that it was at the same hour that Jesus said to him: Thy son liveth. And himself believed, and his whole house. 54 This is again the second miracle that Jesus did, when he was come out of Judea. into Galilee.

JOHN CHAPTER 5

Christ heals on the sabbath the man languishing thirty-eight years. His discourse upon this occasion.

1 After these things was a festival day of the Jews: and Jesus went up to Jerusalem. 2 Now there is at Jerusalem a pond, called Probatica, which in Hebrew is named Bethsaida, having five porches.[7] 3 In these lay a great multitude of sick, of blind, of lame, of withered: waiting for the moving of the water. 4 And an angel of the Lord descended at certain times into

---

7 Probatica... That is, the sheep pond; either so called, because the sheep were washed therein, that were to be offered up in sacrifice in the temple, or because it was near the sheep gate. That this was a pond where miracles were wrought is evident from the sacred text; and also that the water had no natural virtue to heal, as one only of those put in after the motion of the water was restored to health; for if the water had the healing quality, the others would have the like benefit, being put into it about the same time.

the pond and the water was moved. And he that went down first into the pond after the motion of the water was made whole of whatsoever infirmity he lay under. 5 And there was a certain man there that had been eight and thirty years under his infirmity. 6 Him when Jesus had seen lying, and knew that he had been now a long time, he saith to him: Wilt thou be made whole? 7 The infirm man answered him: Sir, I have no man, when the water is troubled, to put me into the pond. For whilst I am coming, another goeth down before me. 8 Jesus saith to him: Arise, take up thy bed and walk. 9 And immediately the man was made whole: and he took up his bed and walked. And it was the sabbath that day. 10 The Jews therefore said to him that was healed: It is the sabbath. It is not lawful for thee to take up thy bed. 11 He answered them: He that made me whole, he said to me: Take up thy bed and walk. 12 They asked him therefore: Who is that man who said to thee: Take up thy bed and walk? 13 But he who was healed knew not who it was: for Jesus went aside from the multitude standing in the place. 14 Afterwards, Jesus findeth him in the temple and saith to him: Behold thou art made whole: sin no more, lest some worse thing happen to thee. 15 The man went his way and told the Jews that it was Jesus who had made him whole. 16 Therefore did the Jews persecute Jesus, because he did these things on the sabbath. 17 But Jesus answered them: My Father worketh until now; and I work. 18 Hereupon therefore the Jews sought the more to kill him, because he did not only break the sabbath but also said God was his Father, making himself equal to God. 19 Then Jesus answered and said to them: Amen, amen, I say unto you, the Son cannot do any thing of himself, but what he seeth the Father doing: for what things soever he doth, these the Son also doth in like manner. 20 For the Father loveth the Son and sheweth him all things which himself doth: and greater works than these will he shew him, that you may wonder. 21 For as the Father raiseth up the dead and giveth life: so the Son also giveth life to whom he will. 22 For neither does the Father judge any man: but hath given all judgment to the Son. 23 That all men may honour the Son, as they honour the Father. He who honoureth not the Son honoureth not the Father who hath sent him. 24 Amen, amen, I say unto you that he who heareth my word and believeth him that sent me hath life everlasting: and cometh not into judgment, but is passed from death to life. 25 Amen, amen, I say unto you, that the hour cometh, and now is, when the dead shall hear the voice of the Son of God: and they that hear shall live. 26 For as the Father hath life in himself, so he hath given to the Son also to have life in himself. 27 And he hath given him power to do judgment, because he is the Son of man. 28 Wonder not at this: for the hour cometh wherein all that are in the graves shall hear the voice of the Son of God. 29 And they that have done good things shall come forth unto the resurrection of life: but they that have done evil, unto the resurrection of judgment.[8] 30 I cannot of myself do any thing. As I hear, so I judge.

8 Unto the resurrection of judgment... That is, condemnation.

And my judgment is just: because I seek not my own will but the will of him that sent me. 31 If I bear witness of myself, my witness is not true. 32 There is another that beareth witness of me: and I know that the witness which he witnesseth of me is true. 33 You sent to John: and he gave testimony to the truth. 34 But I receive not testimony from man: but I say these things, that you may be saved. 35 He was a burning and a shining light: and you were willing for a time to rejoice in his light. 36 But I have a greater testimony than that of John: for the works which the Father hath given me to perfect, the works themselves which I do, give testimony of me, that the Father hath sent me. 37 And the Father himself who hath sent me hath given testimony of me: neither have you heard his voice at any time, nor seen his shape. 38 And you have not his word abiding in you: for whom he hath sent, him you believe not. 39 Search the scriptures: for you think in them to have life everlasting. And the same are they that give testimony of me.[9] 40 And you will not come to me that you may have life. 41 I receive not glory from men. 42 But I know you, that you have not the love of God in you. 43 I am come in the name of my Father, and you receive me not: if another shall come

---

9 Or... You search the scriptures. Scrutamini... It is not a command for all to read the scriptures; but a reproach to the Pharisees, that reading the scriptures as they did, and thinking to find everlasting life in them, they would not receive him to whom all those scriptures gave testimony, and through whom alone they could have that true life.

in his own name, him you will receive. 44 How can you believe, who receive glory one from another: and the glory which is from God alone, you do not seek? 45 Think not that I will accuse you to the Father. There is one that accuseth you, Moses, in whom you trust. 46 For if you did believe Moses, you would perhaps believe me also: for he wrote of me. 47 But if you do not believe his writings, how will you believe my words?

JOHN CHAPTER 6

Christ feeds five thousand with five loaves. He walks upon the sea and discourses of the bread of life.

1After these things Jesus went over the sea of Galilee, which is that of Tiberias. 2 And a great multitude followed him, because they saw the miracles which he did on them that were diseased. 3 Jesus therefore went up into a mountain: and there he sat with his disciples. 4 Now the pasch, the festival day of the Jews, was near at hand. 5 When Jesus therefore had lifted up his eyes and seen that a very great multitude cometh to him, he said to Philip: Whence shall we buy bread, that these may eat? 6 And this he said to try him: for he himself knew what he would do. 7 Philip answered him: Two hundred pennyworth of bread is not sufficient for them that every one may take a little. 8 One of his disciples, Andrew, the brother of Simon Peter, saith to him: 9 There is a boy here that hath five barley loaves and two fishes. But what are these among so many? 10 Then Jesus said: Make the men sit down. Now, there was much grass in the place. The men therefore sat down, in number about five thousand. 11 And Jesus took the loaves: and when he had given thanks, he distributed to them that were set down. In like manner also of the fishes, as much as they would. 12 And when they were filled, he said to his disciples: gather up the fragments that remain, lest they be lost. 13 They gathered up therefore and filled twelve baskets with the fragments of the five barley loaves which remained over and above to them that had eaten. 14 Now those men, when they had seen what a miracle Jesus had done, said: This is of a truth the prophet that is to come into the world. 15 Jesus therefore, when he knew that they would come to take him by force and make him king, fled again into the mountains, himself alone. 16 And when evening was come, his disciples went down to the sea. 17 And when they had gone up into a ship, they went over the sea to Capharnaum. And it was now dark: and Jesus was not come unto them. 18 And the sea arose, by reason of a great wind that blew. 19 When they had rowed therefore about five and twenty or thirty furlongs, they see Jesus walking upon the sea and drawing nigh to the ship. And they were afraid. 20 But he saith to them: It is I. Be not afraid. 21 They were willing therefore to take him into the ship. And presently the ship was at the land to which they were going. 22 The next day, the multitude that stood on the other side of the sea saw that there was no other ship there but one: and that Jesus had not entered into the ship with his disciples, but that his disciples were gone away alone. 23 But other ships came in from Tiberias, nigh unto the place where they had eaten the bread, the Lord giving thanks. 24 When therefore the multitude saw that Jesus was not there, nor his disciples, they took shipping and came to Capharnaum, seeking for Jesus. 25 And when they had found him on that other side of the sea, they said to him: Rabbi, when camest thou hither? 26 Jesus answered them and said: Amen, amen, I say to you, you seek me, not because you have seen miracles, but because you did eat of the loaves and were filled. 27 Labour not for the meat which perisheth, but for that which endureth unto life everlasting, which the Son of man will give you. For him hath God, the Father, sealed. 28 They said therefore unto him: What shall we do, that we may work the works of God? 29 Jesus answered and said to them: This is the work of God, that you believe in him whom he hath sent. 30 They said therefore to him: What sign therefore dost thou shew that we may see and may believe thee? What dost thou work? 31 Our fathers did eat manna in the desert, as it is written: He gave them bread from heaven to eat. 32 Then Jesus said to them: Amen, amen, I say to you; Moses gave you not bread from heaven, but my Father giveth you the true bread from heaven. 33 For the bread of God is that which cometh down from heaven and giveth life to the world. 34 They said therefore unto him: Lord, give us always this bread. 35 And Jesus said to them: I am the bread of life. He that cometh to me shall not hunger: and he that believeth in me shall never thirst. 36 But I said unto you that you also have seen me, and you believe not. 37 All that the Father giveth to me shall come to me: and him that cometh to me, I will not cast out. 38 Because I came down from heaven, not to do my own will but the will of him that sent me. 39 Now this is the will of the Father who sent me: that of all that he hath given me, I should lose nothing; but should raise it up again in the last day. 40 And this is the will of my Father that sent me: that every one who seeth the Son and believeth in him may have life everlasting. And I will raise him up in the last day. 41 The Jews therefore murmured at him, because he had said: I am the living bread which came down from heaven. 42 And they said: Is not this Jesus, the son of Joseph, whose father and mother we know? How then saith he: I came down from heaven? 43 Jesus therefore answered and said to them: Murmur not among yourselves. 44 No man can come to me, except the Father, who hath sent me, draw him. And I will raise him up in the last day.[10] 45 It is written in the prophets: And they shall all be taught of God. Every one that hath heard of the Father and hath learned cometh forth me. 46 Not that any man hath seen the Father: but he who is of God, he hath seen the Father. 47 Amen, amen, I say unto you: He that believeth in me hath everlasting life. 48 I am the bread of life. 49 Your fathers did eat manna in the desert: and are dead. 50

10 Draw him... Not by compulsion, nor by laying the free will under any necessity, but by the strong and sweet motions of his heavenly grace.

This is the bread which cometh down from heaven: that if any man eat of it, he may not die. 51 I am the living bread which came down from heaven. 52 If any man eat of this bread, he shall live for ever: and the bread that I will give is my flesh, for the life of the world. 53 The Jews therefore strove among themselves, saying: How can this man give us his flesh to eat? 54 Then Jesus said to them: Amen, amen, I say unto you: except you eat the flesh of the Son of man and drink his blood, you shall not have life in you.[11] 55 He that eateth my flesh and drinketh my blood hath everlasting life: and I will raise him up in the last day. 56 For my flesh is meat indeed: and my blood is drink indeed. 57 He that eateth my flesh and drinketh my blood abideth in me: and I in him. 58 As the living Father hath sent me and I live by the Father: so he that eateth me, the same also shall live by me. 59 This is the bread that came down from heaven. Not as

---

11 Except you eat and drink, etc... To receive the body and blood of Christ, is a divine precept, insinuated in this text; which the faithful fulfil, though they receive but in one kind; because in one kind they receive both body and blood, which cannot be separated from each other. Hence, life eternal is here promised to the worthy receiving, though but in one kind. Ver. 52. If any man eat of this bread, he shall live for ever; and the bread that I will give, is my flesh for the life of the world. Ver. 58. He that eateth me, the same also shall live by me. Ver. 59. He that eateth this bread, shall liver for ever.

your fathers did eat manna and are dead. He that eateth this bread shall live for ever. 60 These things he said, teaching in the synagogue, in Capharnaum. 61 Many therefore of his disciples, hearing it, said: This saying is hard; and who can hear it? 62 But Jesus, knowing in himself that his disciples murmured at this, said to them: Doth this scandalize you? 63 If then you shall see the Son of man ascend up where he was before?[12] 64 It is the spirit that quickeneth: the flesh profiteth nothing. The words that I have spoken to you are spirit and life.[13] 65 But there are some of you that believe

---

12 If then you shall see, etc... Christ by mentioning his ascension, by this instance of his power and divinity, would confirm the truth of what he had before asserted; and at the same time correct their gross apprehension of eating his flesh, and drinking his blood, in a vulgar and carnal manner, by letting them know he should take his whole body living with him to heaven; and consequently not suffer it to be as they supposed, divided, mangled, and consumed upon earth.

13 The flesh profiteth nothing... Dead flesh separated from the spirit, in the gross manner they supposed they were to eat his flesh, would profit nothing. Neither doth man's flesh, that is to say, man's natural and carnal apprehension, (which refuses to be subject to the spirit, and words of Christ,) profit any thing. But it would be the height of blasphemy, to say the living flesh of Christ (which we receive in the blessed sacarament, with his spirit, that is,

not. For Jesus knew from the beginning who they were that did not believe and who he was that would betray him. 66 And he said: Therefore did I say to you that no man can come to me, unless it be given him by my Father. 67 After this, many of his disciples went back and walked no more with him. 68 Then Jesus said to the twelve: Will you also go away? 69 And Simon Peter answered him: Lord, to whom shall we go? Thou hast the words of eternal life. 70 And we have believed and have known that thou art the Christ, the Son of God. 71 Jesus answered them: Have not I chosen you twelve? And one of you is a devil. 72 Now he meant Judas Iscariot, the son of Simon: for this same was about to betray him, whereas he was one of the twelve.

JOHN CHAPTER 7

Christ goes up to the feast of the tabernacles. He teaches in the temple.

1After these things, Jesus walked in Galilee: for he

with his soul and divinity) profiteth nothing. For if Christ's flesh had profited us nothing, he would never have taken flesh for us, nor died in us nothing, he would never have taken flesh for us, nor died in the flesh for us. Are spirit and life... By proposing to you a heavenly sacrament, in which you shall receive, in a wonderful manner, spirit, grace, and life, in its very fountain.

would not walk in Judea, because the Jews sought to kill him. 2 Now the Jews feast of tabernacles was at hand. 3 And his brethren said to, him: Pass from hence and go into Judea, that thy disciples also may see thy works which thou dost. 4 For there is no man that doth any thing in secret, and he himself seeketh to be known openly. If thou do these things, manifest thyself to the world. 5 For neither did his brethren believe in him. 6 Then Jesus said to them: My time is not yet come; but your time is always ready. 7 The world cannot hate you: but me it hateth, because I give testimony of it, that the works thereof are evil, 8 Go you up to this festival day: but I go not up to this festival day, because my time is not accomplished. 9 When he had said these things, he himself stayed in Galilee. 10 But after his brethren were gone up, then he also went up to the feast, not openly, but, as it were, in secret. 11 The Jews therefore sought him on the festival day and said: Where is he? 12 And there was much murmuring among the multitude concerning him. For some said: He is a good man. And others said: No, but he seduceth the people. 13 Yet no man spoke openly of him, for fear of the Jews. 14 Now, about the midst of the feast, Jesus went up into the temple and taught. 15 And the Jews wondered, saying: How doth this man know letters, having never learned? 16 Jesus answered them and said: My doctrine is not mine, but his that sent me. 17 If any man will do the will of him, he shall know of the doctrine, whether it be of God, or whether I speak of myself. 18 He that speaketh of himself seeketh his own glory: but he that seeketh the glory of him that sent him, he is true and there is no injustice in him. 19 Did not Moses give you the law, and yet none of you keepeth the law? 20 Why seek you to kill me? The multitude answered and said: Thou hast a devil. Who seeketh to kill thee? 21 Jesus answered and said to them: One work I have done: and you all wonder. 22 Therefore, Moses gave you circumcision (not because it is of Moses, but of the fathers): and on the sabbath day you circumcise a man. 23 If a man receive circumcision on the sabbath day, that the law of Moses may not be broken: are you angry at me, because I have healed the whole man on the sabbath day? 24 Judge not according to the appearance: but judge just judgment. 25 Some therefore of Jerusalem said: Is not this he whom they seek to kill? 26 And behold, he speaketh openly: and they say nothing to him. Have the rulers known for a truth that this is the Christ? 27 But we know this man, whence he is: but when the Christ cometh, no man knoweth, whence he is. 28 Jesus therefore cried out in the temple, teaching and saying: You both know me, and you know whence I am. And I am not come of myself: but he that sent me is true, whom you know not. 29 I know him, because I am from him: and he hath sent me. 30 They sought therefore to apprehend him: and no man laid hands on him, because his hour was not yet come. 31 But of the people many believed in him and said: When the Christ cometh, shall he do more miracles than this man doth? 32 The Pharisees heard the people murmuring these things concerning him: and the rulers and Pharisees sent ministers to apprehend him. 33 Jesus therefore said to them: Yet a little while I am with you: and then I go to him that sent me. 34 You shall seek me and shall not find me: and where I am, thither you cannot come. 35 The Jews therefore said among themselves: Whither will he go, that we shall not find him? Will he go unto the dispersed among the Gentiles and teach the Gentiles? 36 What is this saying that he hath said: You shall seek me and shall not find me? And: Where I am, you cannot come? 37 And on the last, and great day of the festivity, Jesus stood and cried, saying: If any man thirst, let him come to me and drink. 38 He that believeth in me, as the scripture saith: Out of his belly shall flow rivers of living water. 39 Now this he said of the Spirit which they should receive who believed in him: for as yet the Spirit was not given, because Jesus was not yet glorified. 40 Of that multitude therefore, when they had heard these words of his, some said: This is the prophet indeed. 41 Others said: This is the Christ. But some said: Doth the Christ come out of Galilee? 42 Doth not the scripture say: That Christ cometh of the seed of David and from Bethlehem the town where David was? 43 So there arose a dissension among the people because of him. 44 And some of them would have apprehended him: but no man laid hands upon him. 45 The ministers therefore came to the chief priests and the Pharisees. And they said to them: Why have you not brought him? 46 The ministers answered: Never did man speak like this man. 47 The Pharisees therefore answered them: Are you also seduced? 48

Hath any one of the rulers believed in him, or of the Pharisees? 49 But this multitude, that knoweth not the law, are accursed. 50 Nicodemus said to them (he that came to him by night, who was one of them): 51 Doth our law judge any man, unless it first hear him and know what he doth? 52 They answered and said to him: Art thou also a Galilean? Search the scriptures, and see that out of Galilee a prophet riseth not. 53 And every man returned to his own house.

JOHN CHAPTER 8

The woman taken in adultery.
Christ justifies his doctrine.

1 And Jesus went unto mount Olivet. 2 And early in the morning he came again into the temple: and all the people came to him. And sitting down he taught them. 3 And the scribes and Pharisees bring unto him a woman taken in adultery: and they set her in the midst, 4 And said to him: Master, this woman was even now taken in adultery. 5 Now Moses in the law commanded us to stone such a one. But what sayest thou? 6 And this they said tempting him, that they might accuse him. But Jesus bowing himself down, wrote with his finger on the ground. 7 When therefore they continued asking him, he lifted up himself and said to them: He that is without sin among you, let him first cast a stone at her. 8 And again stooping down, he wrote on the ground. 9 But they hearing this, went out

one by one, beginning at the eldest. And Jesus alone remained, and the woman standing in the midst. 10 Then Jesus lifting up himself, said to her: Woman, where are they that accused thee? Hath no man condemned thee? 11 Who said: No man, Lord. And Jesus said: Neither will I condemn thee. Go, and now sin no more. 12 Again therefore, Jesus spoke to: them, saying: I am the light of the world. He that followeth me walketh not in darkness, but shall have the light of life. 13 The Pharisees therefore said to him: Thou givest testimony of thyself. Thy testimony is not true. 14 Jesus answered and said to them: Although I give testimony of myself, my testimony is true: for I know whence I came and whither I go. 15 You judge according to the flesh: I judge not any man. 16 And if I do judge, my judgment is true: because I am not alone, but I and the Father that sent me. 17 And in your law it is written that the testimony of two men is true. 18 I am one that give testimony of myself: and the Father that sent me giveth testimony of me. 19 They said therefore to him: Where is thy Father? Jesus answered: Neither me do you know, nor my Father. If you did know me, perhaps you would know my Father also. 20 These words Jesus spoke in the treasury, teaching in the temple: and no man laid hands on him, because his hour was not yet come. 21 Again therefore Jesus said to them: I go: and you shall seek me. And you shall die in your sin. Whither I go, you cannot come. 22 The Jews therefore said: Will he kill himself, because he said: Whither I go you cannot come? 23 And he said to them: You are from beneath: I am from above. You are of this world: I am not of this world. 24 Therefore I said to you that you shall die in your sins. For if you believe not that I am he, you shall die in your sin. 25 They said therefore to him: Who art thou? Jesus said to them: The beginning, who also speak unto you. 26 Many things I have to speak and to judge of you. But he that sent me, is true: and the things I have heard of him, these same I speak in the world. 27 And they understood not that he called God his Father. 28 Jesus therefore said to them: When you shall have lifted up, the Son of man, then shall you know that I am he and that I do nothing of myself. But as the Father hath taught me, these things I speak. 29 And he that sent me is with me: and he hath not left me alone. For I do always the things that please him. 30 When he spoke these things, many believed in him. 31 Then Jesus said to those Jews who believed him: If you continue in my word, you shall be my disciples indeed. 32 And you shall know the truth: and the truth shall make you free. 33 They answered him: We are the seed of Abraham: and we have never been slaves to any man. How sayest thou: You shall be free? 34 Jesus answered them: Amen, amen, I say unto you that whosoever committeth sin is the servant of sin. 35 Now the servant abideth not in the house for ever: but the son abideth for ever. 36 If therefore the son shall make you free, you shall be free indeed. 37 I know that you are the children of Abraham: but you seek to kill me, because my word hath no place in you. 38 I speak that which I have seen with my Father: and you do the things that you have seen with your father. 39

They answered and said to him: Abraham is our father. Jesus saith them: If you be the children of Abraham, do the works of Abraham. 40 But now you seek to kill me, a man who have spoken the truth to you, which I have heard of God. This Abraham did not. 41 You do the works of your father. They said therefore to him: We are not born of fornication: we have one Father, even God. 42 Jesus therefore said to them: If God were your Father, you would indeed love me. For from God I proceeded and came. For I came not of myself: but he sent me. 43 Why do you not know my speech? Because you cannot hear my word. 44 You are of your father the devil: and the desires of your father you will do. He was a murderer from the beginning: and he stood not in the truth, because truth is not in him. When he speaketh a lie, he speaketh of his own: for he is a liar, and the father thereof. 45 But if I say the truth, you believe me not. 46 Which of you shall convince me of sin? If I say the truth to you, why do you not believe me: 47 He that is of God heareth the words of God. Therefore you hear them not, because you are not of God. 48 The Jews therefore answered and said to him: Do not we say well that thou art a Samaritan and hast a devil? 49 Jesus answered: I have not a devil: but I honour my Father. And you have dishonoured me. 50 But I seek not my own glory: there is one that seeketh and judgeth. 51 Amen, amen, I say to you: If any man keep my word, he shall not see death for ever. 52 The Jews therefore said: Now we know that thou hast a devil. Abraham is dead, and the prophets: and thou sayest: If any man keep my word, he shall not taste death for ever. 53 Art thou greater than our father Abraham who is dead? And the prophets are dead. Whom dost thou make thyself? 54 Jesus answered: If I glorify myself, my glory is nothing. It is my Father that glorifieth me, of whom you say that he is your God. 55 And you have not known him: but I know him. And if I shall say that I know him not, I shall be like to you, a liar. But I do know him and do keep his word. 56 Abraham your father rejoiced that he might see my day: he saw it and was glad. 57 The Jews therefore said to him: Thou art not yet fifty years old. And hast thou seen Abraham? 58 Jesus said to them: Amen, amen, I say to you, before Abraham was made, I AM. 59 They took up stones therefore to cast at him. But Jesus hid himself and went out of the temple.

JOHN CHAPTER 9

He gives sight to the man born blind.

1 And Jesus passing by, saw a man who was blind from his birth. 2 And his disciples asked him: Rabbi, who hath sinned, this man or his parents, that he should be born blind? 3 Jesus answered: Neither hath this man sinned, nor his parents; but that the works of God should be made manifest in him. 4 I must work the works of him that sent me, whilst it is day: the night cometh, when no man can work. 5 As long as I am in the world, I am the light of the world. 6 When

he had said these things, he spat on the ground and made clay of the spittle and spread the clay upon his eyes, 7 And said to him: Go, wash in the pool of Siloe, which is interpreted, Sent. He went therefore and washed: and he came seeing. 8 The neighbours, therefore, and they who had seen him before that he was a beggar, said: Is not this he that sat and begged? Some said: This is he. 9 But others said: No, but he is like him. But he said: I am he. 10 They said therefore to him: How were thy eyes opened? 11 He answered: That man that is called Jesus made clay and anointed my eyes and said to me: Go to the pool of Siloe and wash. And I went: I washed: and I see. 12 And they said to him: Where is he? He saith: I know not. 13 They bring him that had been blind to the Pharisees. 14 Now it was the sabbath, when Jesus made the clay and opened his eyes. 15 Again therefore the Pharisees asked him how he had received his sight. But he said to them: He put clay upon my eyes: and I washed: and I see. 16 Some therefore of the Pharisees said: This man is not of God, who keepeth not the sabbath. But others said: How can a man that is a sinner do such miracles? And there was a division among them. 17 They say therefore to the blind man again: What sayest thou of him that hath opened thy eyes? And he said: He is a prophet. 18 The Jews then did not believe concerning him, that he had been blind and had received his sight, until they called the parents of him that had received his sight, 19 And asked them, saying: Is this your son, who you say was born blind? How then doth he now see? 20 His parents answered them and said: We know that this is our son and that he was born blind: 21 But how he now seeth, we know not: or who hath opened his eyes, we know not. Ask himself: he is of age: Let him speak for himself. 22 These things his parents said, because they feared the Jews: for the Jews had already agreed among themselves that if any man should confess him to be Christ, he should be put out of the synagogue. 23 Therefore did his parents say: He is of age. Ask himself. 24 They therefore called the man again that had been blind and said to him: Give glory to God. We know that this man is a sinner. 25 He said therefore to them: If he be a sinner, I know not. One thing I know, that whereas I was blind now I see. 26 They said then to him: What did he to thee? How did he open thy eyes? 27 He answered them: I have told you already, and you have heard. Why would you hear it again? Will you also become his disciples? 28 They reviled him therefore and said: Be thou his disciple; but we are the disciples of Moses. 29 We know that God spoke to Moses: but as to this man, we know not from whence he is. 30 The man answered and said to them: why, herein is a wonderful thing, that you know not from whence he is, and he hath opened my eyes. 31 Now we know that God doth not hear sinners: but if a man be a server of God and doth his, will, him he heareth. 32 From the beginning of the world it hath not been heard, that any man hath opened the eyes of one born blind. 33 Unless this man were of God, he could not do anything. 34 They answered and said to him: Thou wast wholly born in sins; and dost thou teach us?

And they cast him out. 35 Jesus heard that they had cast him out. And when he had found him, he said to him: Dost thou believe in the Son of God? 36 He answered, and said: Who is he, Lord, that I may believe in him? 37 And Jesus said to him: Thou hast both seen him; and it is he that talketh with thee. 38 And he said: I believe, Lord. And falling down, he adored him. 39 And Jesus said: For judgment I am come into this world: that they who see not may see; and they who see may become blind.[14] 40 And some of the Pharisees, who were with him, heard: and they said unto him: Are we also blind? 41 Jesus said to them: If you were blind, you should not have sin: but now you say: We see. Your sin remaineth.[15]

JOHN CHAPTER 10

Christ is the door and the good shepherd.
He and his Father are one.

---

14 I am come, etc... Not that Christ came for that end, that any one should be made blind: but that the Jews, by the abuse of his coming, and by their not receiving him, brought upon themselves this judgment of blindness.

15 If you were blind, etc... If you were invincibly ignorant, and had neither read the scriptures, nor seen my miracles, you would not be guilty of the sin of infidelity: but now, as you boast of your knowledge of the scriptures, you are inexcusable.

1 Amen, amen, I say to you: He that entereth not by the door into the sheepfold but climbeth up another way, the same is a thief and a robber. 2 But he that entereth in by the door is the shepherd of the sheep. 3 To him the porter openeth: and the sheep hear his voice. And he calleth his own sheep by name and leadeth them out. 4 And when he hath let out his own sheep, he goeth before them: and the sheep follow him, because they know his voice. 5 But a stranger they follow not, but fly from him, because theyknow not the voice of strangers. 6 This proverb Jesus spoke to them. But they understood not what he spoke. 7 Jesus therefore said to them again: Amen, amen, I say to you, I am the door of the sheep. 8 All others, as many as have come, are thieves and robbers: and the sheep heard them not. 9 I am the door. By me, if any man enter in, he shall be saved: and he shall go in and go out, and shall find pastures. 10 The thief cometh not, but for to steal and to kill and to destroy. I am come that they may have life and may have it more abundantly. 11 I am the good shepherd. The good shepherd giveth his life for his sheep. 12 But the hireling and he that is not the shepherd, whose own the sheep are not, seeth the wolf coming and leaveth the sheep and flieth: and the wolf casteth and scattereth the sheep, 13And the hireling flieth, because he is a hireling: and he hath no care for the sheep. 14 I am the good shepherd: and I know mine, and mine know me. 15 As the Father knoweth me, and I know the Father: and I lay down my life for my sheep. 16 And other

sheep I have that are not of this fold: them also I must bring. And they shall hear my voice: And there shall be one fold and one shepherd. 17 Therefore doth the Father love me: because I lay down my life, that I may take it again. 18 No man taketh it away from me: but I lay it down of myself. And I have power to lay it down: and I have power to take it up again. This commandment have I received of my Father. 19 A dissension rose again among the Jews for these words. 20 And many of them said: He hath a devil and is mad. Why hear you him? 21 Others said: These are not the words of one that hath a devil. Can a devil open the eyes of the blind? 22 And it was the feast of the dedication at Jerusalem: and it was winter. 23 And Jesus walked in the temple, in Solomon's porch. 24 The Jews therefore came round about him and said to him: How long dost thou hold our souls in suspense? If thou be the Christ, tell us plainly. 25 Jesus answered them: I speak to you, and you believe not: the works that I do in the name of my Father, they give testimony of me. 26 But you do not believe, because you are not of my sheep. 27 My sheep hear my voice. And I know them: and they follow me. 28 And I give them life everlasting: and they shall not perish for ever. And no man shall pluck them out of my hand. 29 That which my Father hath given me is greater than all: and no one can snatch them out of the hand of my Father. 30 I and the Father are one.[16] 31 The Jews then took up stones to stone him. 32 Jesus answered them:

16 I and the Father are one... That is, one divine nature, but two distinct persons.

Many good works I have shewed you from my Father. For which of those works do you stone me? 33 The Jews answered him: For a good work we stone thee not, but for blasphemy: and because that thou being a, man, makest thyself God. 34 Jesus answered them: Is it not written in your law: I said, you are gods? 35 If he called them gods to whom the word of God was spoken; and the scripture cannot be broken: 36 Do you say of him whom the Father hath sanctified and sent into the world: Thou blasphemest; because I said: I am the Son of God? 37 If I do not the works of my Father, believe me not. 38 But if I do, though you will not believe me, believe the works: that you may know and believe that the Father is in me and I in the Father. 39 They sought therefore to take him: and he escaped out of their hands. 40 And he went again beyond the Jordan, into that place where John was baptizing first. And there he abode. 41 And many resorted to him: and they said: John indeed did no sign. 42 But all things whatsoever John said of this man were true. And many believed in him.

JOHN CHAPTER 11

Christ raises Lazarus to life.
The rulers resolve to put him to death.

1 Now there was a certain man sick, named Lazarus, of Bethania, of the town of Mary and of Martha her sister. 2 (And Mary was she that anointed the Lord

with ointment and wiped his feet with her hair: whose brother Lazarus was sick.) 3 His sisters therefore sent to him, saying: Lord, behold, he whom thou lovest is sick. 4 And Jesus hearing it, said to them: This sickness is not unto death, but for the glory of God: that the Son of God may be glorified by it. 5 Now Jesus loved Martha and her sister Mary and Lazarus. 6 When he had heard therefore that he was sick, he still remained in the same place two days. 7 Then after that, he said to his disciples: Let us go into Judea again. 8 The disciples say to him: Rabbi, the Jews but now sought to stone thee. And goest thou thither again? 9 Jesus answered: Are there not twelve hours of the day? If a man walk in the day he stumbleth not, because he seeth the light of this world: 10 But if he walk in the night, he stumbleth, because the light is not in him. 11 These things he said; and after that he said to them: Lazarus our friend sleepeth: but I go that I may awake him out of sleep. 12 His disciples therefore said: Lord, if he sleep, he shall do well. 13 But Jesus spoke of his death: and they thought that he spoke of the repose of sleep. 14 Then therefore Jesus said to them plainly: Lazarus is dead. 15 And I am glad, for your sakes; that I was not there, that you may believe. But, let us go to him. 16 Thomas therefore, who is called Didymus, said to his fellow disciples: Let us also go, that we may die with him. 17 Jesus therefore came: and found that he had been four days already in the grave. 18 (Now Bethania was near Jerusalem, about fifteen furlongs off.) 19 And many of the Jews were come to Martha and Mary, to comfort them concerning their brother. 20 Martha therefore, as soon as she heard that Jesus was come, went to meet him: but Mary sat at home. 21 Martha therefore said to Jesus: Lord, if thou hadst been here, my brother had not died. 22 But now also I know that whatsoever thou wilt ask of God, God will give it thee. 23 Jesus saith to her: Thy brother shall rise again. 24 Martha saith to him: I know that he shall rise again, in the resurrection at the last day. 25 Jesus said to her: I am the resurrection and the life: he that believeth in me, although he be dead, shall live: 26 And every one that liveth and believeth in me shall not die for ever. Believest thou this? 27 She saith to him: Yea, Lord, I have believed that thou art Christ, the Son of the living God, who art come into this world. 28 And when she had said these things, she went and called her sister Mary secretly, saying: The master is come and calleth for thee. 29 She, as soon as she heard this, riseth quickly and cometh to him. 30 For Jesus was not yet come into the town: but he was still in that place where Martha had met him. 31 The Jews therefore, who were with her in the house and comforted her, when they saw Mary, that she rose up speedily and went out, followed her, saying: She goeth to the grave to weep there. 32 When Mary therefore was come where Jesus was, seeing him, she fell down at his feet and saith to him. Lord, if thou hadst been here, my brother had not died. 33 Jesus, therefore, when he saw her weeping, and the Jews that were come with her weeping, groaned in the spirit and troubled himself, 34 And said: Where have you laid him? They say to him:

Lord, come and see. 35 And Jesus wept. 36 The Jews therefore said: Behold how he loved him. 37 But some of them said: Could not he that opened the eyes of the man born blind have caused that this man should not die? 38 Jesus therefore again groaning in himself, cometh to the sepulchre. Now it was a cave; and a stone was laid over it. 39 Jesus saith: Take away the stone. Martha, the sister of him that was dead, saith to him: Lord, by this time he stinketh, for he is now of four days. 40 Jesus saith to her: Did not I say to thee that if thou believe, thou shalt see the glory of God? 41 They took therefore the stone away. And Jesus lifting up his eyes, said: Father, I give thee thanks that thou hast heard me. 42 And I knew that thou hearest me always: but because of the people who stand about have I said it, that they may believe that thou hast sent me. 43 When he had said these things, he cried with a loud voice: Lazarus, come forth. 44 And presently he that had been dead came forth, bound feet and hands with winding bands. And his face was bound about with a napkin. Jesus said to them: Loose him and let him go. 45 Many therefore of the Jews, who were come to Mary and Martha and had seen the things that Jesus did, believed in him. 46 But some of them went to the Pharisees and told them the things that Jesus had done. 47 The chief priests, therefore, and the Pharisees gathered a council and said: What do we, for this man doth many miracles? 48 If we let him alone so, all will believe in him; and the Romans will come, and take away our place and nation. 49 But one of them, named Caiphas, being the high priest that year, said to them:

You know nothing. 50 Neither do you consider that it is expedient for you that one man should die for the people and that the whole nation perish not. 51 And this he spoke not of himself: but being the high priest of that year, he prophesied that Jesus should die for the nation. 52 And not only for the nation, but to gather together in one the children of God that were dispersed. 53 From that day therefore they devised to put him to death. 54 Wherefore Jesus walked no more openly among the Jews: but he went into a country near the desert, unto a city that is called Ephrem. And there he abode with his disciples. 55 And the pasch of the Jews was at hand: and many from the country went up to Jerusalem, before the pasch, to purify themselves. 56 They sought therefore for Jesus; and they discoursed one with another, standing in the temple: What think you that he is not come to the festival day? And the chief priests and Pharisees had given a commandment that, if any man knew where he was, he should tell, that they might apprehend him.

JOHN CHAPTER 12

The anointing of Christ's feet. His riding into Jerusalem upon an ass. A voice from heaven.

1 Jesus therefore, six days before the pasch, came to Bethania, where Lazarus had been dead, whom Jesus raised to life. 2 And they made him a supper there: and Martha served. But Lazarus was one of them that were

at table with him. 3 Mary therefore took a pound of ointment of right spikenard, of great price, and anointed the feet of Jesus and wiped his feet with her hair. And the house was filled with the odour of the ointment. 4 Then one of his disciples, Judas Iscariot, he that was about to betray him, said: 5 Why was not this ointment sold for three hundred pence and given to the poor? 6 Now he said this not because he cared for the poor; but because he was a thief and, having the purse, carried the things that were put therein. 7 Jesus therefore said: Let her alone, that she may keep it against the day of my burial. 8 For the poor you have always with you: but me you have not always.[17] 9 A great multitude therefore of the Jews knew that he was there; and they came, not for Jesus' sake only, but that they might see Lazarus, whom he had raised from the dead. 10 But the chief priests thought to kill Lazarus also: 11 Because many of the Jews, by reason of him, went away and believed in Jesus. 12 And on the next day, a great multitude that was come to the festival day, when they had heard that Jesus was coming to Jerusalem, 13 Took branches of palm trees and went forth to meet him and cried Hosanna. Blessed is he that cometh in the name of the Lord, the king of Israel. 14 And Jesus found a young ass and sat upon it, as it is written: 15 Fear not, daughter of Sion: behold thy king cometh, sitting on an ass's colt. 16 These things his disciples did not know at the first: but when Jesus was glorified, then they remembered that these things were written of him and that they had

---

17 See the annotation of St. Matt. 26. 11.

done these things to him. 17 The multitude therefore gave testimony, which was with him, when he called Lazarus out of the grave and raised him from the dead. 18 For which reason also the people came to meet him, because they heard that he had done this miracle. 19 The Pharisees therefore said among themselves: Do you see that we prevail nothing? Behold, the whole world is gone after him. 20 Now there were certain Gentiles among them, who came up to adore on the festival day. 21 These therefore came to Philip, who was of Bethsaida of Galilee, and desired him, saying: Sir, we would see Jesus. 22 Philip cometh and telleth Andrew. Again Andrew and Philip told Jesus. 23 But Jesus answered them, saying: The hour is come that the Son of man should be glorified. 24 Amen, amen, I say to you, unless the grain of wheat falling into the ground die, 25 Itself remaineth alone. But if it die it bringeth forth much fruit. He that loveth his life shall lose it and he that hateth his life in this world keepeth it unto life eternal. 26 If any man minister to me, let him follow me: and where I am, there also shall my minister be. If any man minister to me, him will my Father honour. 27 Now is my soul troubled. And what shall I say? Father, save me from this hour. But for this cause I came unto this hour. 28 Father, glorify thy name. A voice therefore came from heaven: I have both glorified it and will glorify it again. 29 The multitude therefore that stood and heard said that it thundered. Others said: An angel spoke to him. 30 Jesus answered and said: This voice came not because of me, but for your sakes. 31 Now is the judgment of the world: now shall the prince of this world be cast out. 32 And I, if I be lifted up from the earth, will draw all things to myself. 33 (Now this he said, signifying what death he should die.) 34 The multitude answered him: We have heard out of the law that Christ abideth for ever. And how sayest thou: The Son of man must be lifted up? Who is this Son of man? 35 Jesus therefore said to them: Yet a little while, the light is among you. Walk whilst you have the light, and the darkness overtake you not. And he that walketh in darkness knoweth not whither be goeth. 36 Whilst you have the light, believe in the light, that you may be the children of light. These things Jesus spoke: and he went away and hid himself from them. 37 And whereas he had done so many miracles before them, they believed not in him: 38 That the saying of Isaias the prophet might be fulfilled, which he said: Lord, who hath believed our hearing? And to whom hath the arm of the Lord been revealed? 39 Therefore they could not believe, because Isaias said again:[18] 40 He hath blinded their eyes and hardened their heart, that they should not see with their eyes, nor understand with their heart and be converted: and I should heal them. 41 These things said Isaias, when he saw his glory, and spoke of him. 42 However, many of the chief men also believed in him: but because of the Pharisees they did not confess him, that they might not be cast out of the synagogue. 43 For they loved the

18 They could not believe... Because they would not, saith St. Augustine, Tract. 33, in Joan. See the annotation, St. Mark 4. 12.

glory of men more than the glory of God. 44 But Jesus cried and said: He that believeth in me doth not believe in me, but in him that sent me. 45 And he that seeth me, seeth him that sent me. 46 I am come, a light into the world, that whosoever believeth in me may not remain in darkness. 47 And if any man hear my words and keep them not, I do not judge him for I came not to judge the world, but to save the world. 48 He that despiseth me and receiveth not my words hath one that judgeth him. The word that I have spoken, the same shall judge him in the last day. 49 For I have not spoken of myself: but the Father who sent me, he gave me commandment what I should say and what I should speak. 50 And I know that his commandment is life everlasting. The things therefore that I speak, even as the Father said unto me, so do I speak.

JOHN CHAPTER 13

Christ washes his disciples' feet. The treason of Judas. The new commandment of love.

1 Before the festival day of the pasch, Jesus knowing that his hour was come, that he should pass out of this world to the Father: having loved his own who were in the world, he loved them unto the end.[19] 2 And when

19 Before the festival day of the pasch... This was the fourth and last pasch of the ministry of Christ, and according to the common computation, was in the thirty-third year of our Lord: and in the year of the

supper was done (the devil having now put into the heart of Judas Iscariot, the son of Simon, to betray him), 3 Knowing that the Father had given him all things into his hands and that he came from God and goeth to God, 4 He riseth from supper and layeth aside his garments and, having taken a towel, girded himself. 5 After that, he putteth water into a basin and began to wash the feet of the disciples and to wipe them with the towel wherewith he was girded. 6 He cometh therefore to Simon Peter. And Peter saith to him: Lord, dost thou wash my feet? 7 Jesus answered and said to him: What I do, thou knowest not now; but thou shalt know hereafter. 8 Peter saith to him: Thou shalt never wash my feet, Jesus answered him: If I wash thee not, thou shalt have no part with me. 9 Simon Peter saith to him: Lord, not only my feet, but also my hands and my head. 10 Jesus saith to him: He that is washed needeth not but to wash his feet, but is clean wholly. And you are clean, but not all. 11 For he knew who he was that would betray him; therefore he said: You are not all clean. 12 Then after he had washed their feet and taken his garments, being set down again, he said to them: Know you what I have done to you? 13 You call me Master and Lord. And you say well: for so I am. 14 If then I being your Lord and Master, have washed your feet; you also ought to wash one another's feet. 15 For I have given you an

world 4036. Some chronologers are of opinion that our Saviour suffered in the thirty-seventh year of his age: but these different opinions on this subject are of no consequence.

example, that as I have done to you, so you do also. 16 Amen, amen, I say to you: The servant is not greater than his lord: neither is the apostle greater than he that sent him. 17 If you know these things, you shall be blessed if you do them. 18 I speak not of you all: I know whom I have chosen. But that the scripture may be fulfilled: He that eateth bread with me shall lift up his heel against me, 19 At present I tell you, before it come to pass: that when it shall come to pass, you may believe that I am he. 20 Amen, amen, I say to you, he that receiveth whomsoever I send receiveth me: and he that receiveth me receiveth him that sent me. 21 When Jesus had said these things, he was troubled in spirit; and he testified, and said: Amen, amen, I say to you, one of you shall betray me. 22 The disciples therefore looked one upon another, doubting of whom he spoke. 23 Now there was leaning on Jesus' bosom one of his disciples, whom Jesus loved. 24 Simon Peter therefore beckoned to him and said to him: Who is it of whom he speaketh? 25 He therefore, leaning on the breast of Jesus, saith to him: Lord, who is it? 26 Jesus answered: He it is to whom I shall reach bread dipped. And when he had dipped the bread, he gave it to Judas Iscariot, the son of Simon. 27 And after the morsel, Satan entered into him. And Jesus said to him: That which thou dost, do quickly.[20] 28 Now no man at the

---

20 That which thou dost, do quickly... It is not a license, much less a command, to go about his treason: but a signification to him that Christ would not hinder or resist what he was about, do it as soon as he pleased: but was both ready and desirous to

table knew to what purpose he said this unto him. 29 For some thought, because Judas had the purse, that Jesus had said to him: Buy those things which we have need of for the festival day: or that he should give something to the poor. 30 He therefore, having received the morsel, went out immediately. And it was night. 31 When he therefore was gone out, Jesus said: Now is the Son of man glorified; and God is glorified in him. 32 If God be glorified in him, God also will glorify him in himself: and immediately will he glorify him. 33 Little children, yet a little while I am with you. You shall seek me. And as I said to the Jews: Whither I go you cannot come; so I say to you now. 34 A new commandment I give unto you: That you love one another, as I have loved you, that you also love one another. 35 By this shall all men know that you are my disciples, if you have love one for another. 36 Simon Peter saith to him: Lord, whither goest thou? Jesus answered: Whither I go, thou canst not follow me now: but thou shalt follow hereafter. 37 Peter saith to him: Why cannot I follow thee now? I will lay down my life for thee. 38 Jesus answered him: Wilt thou lay down thy life for me? Amen, amen, I say to thee, the cock shall not crow, till thou deny me thrice.

JOHN CHAPTER 14

Christ's discourse after his last supper.

---

suffer for our redemption.

1 Let not your heart be troubled. You believe in God: believe also in me. 2 In my Father's house there are many mansions. If not, I would have told you: because I go to prepare a place for you. 3 And if I shall go and prepare a place for you, I will come again and will take you to myself: that where I am, you also may be. 4 And whither I go you know: and the way you know. 5 Thomas saith to him: Lord, we know not whither thou goest. And how can we know the way? 6 Jesus saith to him: I am the way, and the truth, and the life. No man cometh to the Father, but by me. 7 If you had known me, you would without doubt have known my Father also: and from henceforth you shall know him. And you have seen him. 8 Philip saith to him: Lord, shew us the Father; and it is enough for us. 9 Jesus saith to him: Have I been so long a time with you and have you not known me? Philip, he that seeth me seeth the Father also. How sayest thou: Shew us the Father? 10 Do you not believe that I am in the Father and the Father in me? The words that I speak to you, I speak not of myself. But the Father who abideth in me, he doth the works. 11 Believe you not that I am in the Father and the Father in me? 12 Otherwise believe for the very works' sake. Amen, amen, I say to you, he that believeth in me, the works that I do, he also shall do: and greater than these shall he do. 13 Because I go to the Father: and whatsoever you shall ask the Father in my name, that will I do: that the Father may be glorified in the Son. 14 If you shall ask me any thing in my name, that I will do. 15 If you love me, keep my commandments. 16 And I will ask the Father: and he

shall give you another Paraclete, that he may abide with you for ever:[21] 17 The spirit of truth, whom the world cannot receive, because it seeth him not, nor knoweth him. But you shall know him; because he shall abide with you and shall be in you. 18 I will not leave you orphans: I will come to you. 19 Yet a little while and the world seeth me no more. But you see me: because I live, and you shall live. 20 In that day you shall know that I am in my Father: and you in me, and I in you. 21 He that hath my commandments and keepeth them; he it is that loveth me. And he that loveth me shall be loved of my Father: and I will love him and will manifest myself to him. 22 Judas saith to him, not the Iscariot: Lord, how is it that thou wilt manifest thyself to us, and not to the world? 23 Jesus answered and said to him: If any one love me, he will keep my word. And my Father will love him and we will come to him and will make our abode with him. 24 He that loveth me not keepeth not my words. And the word which you have heard is not mine; but the Father's who sent me. 25 These things have I spoken to you, abiding with you. 26 But the Paraclete, the Holy Ghost, whom the Father will send in my name, he will teach you all things and bring all things to your

---

21 Paraclete... That is, a comforter: or also an advocate; inasmuch as by inspiring prayer, he prays, as it were, in us, and pleads for us. For ever... Hence it is evident that this Spirit of Truth was not only promised to the persons of the apostles, but also to their successors through all generations.

mind, whatsoever I shall have said to you.[22] 27 Peace I leave with you: my peace I give unto you: not as the world giveth, do I give unto you. Let not your heart be troubled: nor let it be afraid. 28 You have heard that I said to you: I go away, and I come unto you. If you loved me you would indeed be glad, because I go to the Father: for the Father is greater than I.[23] 29 And now I have told you before it come to pass: that when it shall come to pass, you may believe. 30 I will not now speak many things with you. For the prince of this world: cometh: and in me he hath not any thing.

---

22 Teach you all things... Here the Holy Ghost is promised to the apostles and their successors, particularly, in order to teach them all truth, and to preserve them from error.

23 For the Father is greater than I... It is evident, that Christ our Lord speaks here of himself as he is made man: for as God he is equal to the Father. (See Phil. 2.) Any difficulty of understanding the meaning of these words will vanish, when the relative circumstances of the text here are considered: for Christ being at this time shortly to suffer death, signified to his apostles his human nature by these very words: for as God he could not die. And therefore as he was both God and man, it must follow that according to his humanity he was to die, which the apostles were soon to see and believe, as he expresses, ver. 29. And now I have told you before it come to pass: that when it shall come to pass, you may believe.

31 But that the world may know that I love the Father: and as the Father hath given me commandments, so do I. Arise, let us go hence.

JOHN CHAPTER 15

A continuation of Christ's discourse to his disciples.

1 I am the true vine: and my Father is the husbandman. 2 Every branch in me that beareth not fruit, he will take away: and every one that beareth fruit, he will purge it, that it may bring forth more fruit. 3 Now you are clean, by reason of the word which I have spoken to you. 4 Abide in me: and I in you. As the branch cannot bear fruit of itself, unless it abide in the vine, so neither can you, unless you abide in me. 5 I am the vine: you the branches. He that abideth in me, and I in him, the same beareth much fruit: for without me you can do nothing. 6 If any one abide not in me, he shall be cast forth as a branch and shall wither: and they shall gather him up and cast him into the fire: and he burneth. 7 If you abide in me and my words abide in you, you shall ask whatever you will: and it shall be done unto you. 8 In this is my Father glorified: that you bring forth very much fruit and become my disciples. 9 As the Father hath loved me, I also have loved you. Abide in my love. 10 If you keep my commandments, you shall abide in my love: as I also have kept my Father's commandments and do abide in his love. 11 These things I have spoken to

you, that my joy may be in you, and your joy may be filled. 12 This is my commandment, that you love one another, as I have loved you. 13 Greater love than this no man hath, that a man lay down his life for his friends. 14 You are my friends, if you do the things that I command you. 15 I will not now call you servants: for the servant knoweth not what his lord doth. But I have called you friends because all things, whatsoever I have heard of my Father, I have made known to you. 16 You have not chosen me: but I have chosen you; and have appointed you, that you should go and should bring forth fruit; and your fruit should remain: that whatsoever you shall ask of the Father in my name, he may give it you. 17 These things I command you, that you love one another. 18 If the world hate you, know ye that it hath hated me before you. 19 If you had been of the world, the world would love its own: but because you are not of the world, but I have chosen you out of the world, therefore the world hateth you. 20 Remember my word that I said to you: The servant is not greater than his master. If they have persecuted me, they will also persecute you. If they have kept my word, they will keep yours also. 21 But all these things they will do to you for my name's sake: because they know not him that sent me. 22 If I had not come and spoken to them, they would not have sin: but now they have no excuse for their sin. 23 He that hateth me hateth my Father also. 24 If I had not done among them the works that no other man hath done, they would not have sin: but now they have both seen and hated both me and my Father. 25 But that the word may be fulfilled which is written in their law: they hated me without cause. 26 But when the Paraclete cometh, whom I will send you from the Father, the Spirit of truth, who proceedeth from the Father, he shall give testimony of me.[24] 27 And you shall give testimony, because you are with me from the beginning.

JOHN CHAPTER 16

The conclusion of Christ's last discourse
to his disciples.

1 These things have I spoken to you things have I spoken to you that you may not be scandalized. 2 They will put you out of the synagogues: yea, the hour cometh, that whosoever killeth you will think that he doth a service to God. 3 And these things will they do to you; because they have not known the Father nor me. 4 But these things I have told you, that when the hour shall come, you may remember that I told you of them. 5 But I told you not these things from the beginning, because I was with you. And now I go to him that sent me, and none of you asketh me: Whither goest thou? 6 But because I have spoken these things

---

24 Whom I will send... This proves, against the modern Greeks, that the Holy Ghost proceedeth from the Son, as well as from the Father: otherwise he could not be sent by the Son.

to you, sorrow hath filled your heart. 7 But I tell you the truth: it is expedient to you that I go. For if I go not, the Paraclete will not come to you: but if I go, I will send him to you. 8 And when he is come, he will convince the world of sin and of justice and of judgment.[25] 9 Of sin: because they believed not in me. 10 And of justice: because I go to the Father: and you shall see me no longer. 11 And of judgment: because the prince of this world is already judged. 12 I have yet many things to say to you: but you cannot bear them now. 13 But when he, the Spirit of truth, is come, he will teach you all truth. For he shall not speak of himself: but what things soever he shall hear, he shall speak. And the things that are to come, he shall shew you.[26] 14 He shall glorify me: because he shall receive of mine and shall shew it to you. 15 All things whatsoever the Father hath are mine. Therefore I said that he shall receive of me and shew it to you. 16 A little while, and now you shall not see me: and again a little while, and you shall see me: because I go to the

---

25 He will convince the world of sin, etc... The Holy Ghost, by his coming brought over many thousands, first, to a sense of their sin in not believing in Christ. Secondly, to a conviction of the justice of Christ, now sitting at the right hand of his Father. And thirdly, to a right apprehension of the judgment prepared for them that choose to follow Satan, who is already judged and condemned.

26 Will teach you all truth... See the annotation on chap. 14. ver. 26.

Father. 17 Then some of his disciples said one to another: What is this that he saith to us: A little while, and you shall not see me: and again a little while, and you shall see me, and, Because I go to the Father? 18 They said therefore: What is this that he saith, A little while? We know not what he speaketh. 19 And Jesus knew that they had a mind to ask him. And he said to them: Of this do you inquire among yourselves, because I said: A little while, and you shall not see me; and again a little while, and you shall see me? 20 Amen, amen, I say to you, that you shall lament and weep, but the world shall rejoice: and you shall be made sorrowful, but your sorrow shall be turned into joy. 21 A woman, when she is in labour, hath sorrow, because her hour is come; but when she hath brought forth the child, she remembereth no more the anguish, for joy that a man is born into the world. 22 So also you now indeed have sorrow: but I will see you again and your heart shall rejoice. And your joy no man shall take from you. 23 And in that day you shall not ask me any thing. Amen, amen, I say to you: if you ask the Father any thing in my name, he will give it you. 24 Hitherto, you have not asked any thing in my name. Ask, and you shall receive; that your joy may be full. 25 These things I have spoken to you in proverbs. The hour cometh when I will no longer speak to you in proverbs, but will shew you plainly of the Father. 26 In that day, you shall ask in my name: and I say not to you that I will ask the Father for you. 27 For the Father himself loveth you, because you have loved me and have believed that I came out from God. 28 I came forth from the Father and am come into the world: again I leave the world and I go to the Father. 29 His disciples say to him: Behold, now thou speakest plainly and speakest no proverb. 30 Now we know that thou knowest all things and thou needest not that any man should ask thee. By this we believe that thou camest forth from God. 31 Jesus answered them: Do you now believe? 32 Behold, the hour cometh, and it is now come, that you shall be scattered every man to his own and shall leave me alone. And yet I am not alone, because the Father is with me. 33 These things I have spoken to you, that in me you may have peace. In the world you shall have distress. But have confidence. I have overcome the world.

JOHN CHAPTER 17

Christ's prayer for his disciples.

1 These things Jesus spoke: and lifting up his eyes to heaven, he said: the hour is come. Glorify thy Son, that thy Son may glorify thee. 2 As thou hast given him power over all flesh, that he may give eternal life to all whom thou hast given him. 3 Now this is eternal life: That they may know thee, the only true God, and Jesus Christ, whom thou hast sent. 4 I have glorified thee on the earth; I have finished the work which thou gavest me to do. 5 And now glorify thou me, O Father, with thyself, with the glory which I had, before the world was, with thee. 6 I have manifested thy name to

the men whom thou hast given me out of the world. Thine they were: and to me thou gavest them. And they have kept thy word. 7 Now they have known that all things which thou hast given me are from thee: 8 Because the words which thou gavest me, I have given to them. And they have received them and have known in very deed that I came out from thee: and they have believed that thou didst send me. 9 I pray for them. I pray not for the world, but for them whom thou hast given me: because they are thine. 10 And all my things are thine, and thine are mine: and I am glorified in them. 11 And now I am not in the world, and these are in the world, and I come to thee. Holy Father, keep them in thy name whom thou hast given me: that they may be one, as we also are. 12 While I was with them, I kept them in thy name. Those whom thou gavest me have I kept: and none of them is lost, but the son of perdition: that the scripture may be fulfilled. 13 And now I come to thee: and these things I speak in the world, that they may have my joy filled in themselves. 14 I have given them thy word, and the world hath hated them: because they are not of the world, as I also am not of the world. 15 I pray not that thou shouldst take them out of the world, but that thou shouldst keep them from evil. 16 They are not of the world, as I also am not of the world. 17 Sanctify them in truth. Thy word is truth. 18 As thou hast sent me into the world, I also have sent them into the world. 19 And for them do I sanctify myself, that they also may be sanctified in truth. 20 And not for them only do I pray, but for them also who through their word shall believe in me.

21 That they all may be one, as thou, Father, in me, and I in thee; that they also may be one in us: that the world may believe that thou hast sent me. 22 And the glory which thou hast given me, I have given to them: that, they may be one, as we also are one. 23 I in them, and thou in me: that they may be made perfect in one: and the world may know that thou hast sent me and hast loved them, as thou hast also loved me. 24 Father, I will that where I am, they also whom thou hast given me may be with me: that they may see my glory which thou hast given me, because thou hast loved me before the creation of the world. 25 Just Father, the world hath not known thee: but I have known thee. And these have known that thou hast sent me. 26 And I have made known thy name to them and will make it known: that the love wherewith thou hast loved me may be in them, and I in them.

JOHN CHAPTER 18

The history of the passion of Christ.

1 When Jesus had said these things, he went forth with his disciples over the brook Cedron, where there was a garden, into which he entered with his disciples. 2 And Judas also, who betrayed him, knew the place: because Jesus had often resorted thither together with his disciples. 3 Judas therefore having received a band of soldiers and servants from the chief priests and the Pharisees, cometh thither with lanterns and torches and

weapons. 4 Jesus therefore, knowing all things that should come upon him, went forth and said to them: Whom seek ye? 5 They answered him: Jesus of Nazareth. Jesus saith to them: I am he. And Judas also, who betrayed him, stood with them. 6 As soon therefore as he had said to them: I am he; they went backward and fell to the ground. 7 Again therefore he asked them: Whom seek ye? And they said: Jesus of Nazareth. 8 Jesus answered: I have told you that I am he. If therefore you seek me, let these go their way, 9 That the word might be fulfilled which he said: Of them whom thou hast given me, I have not lost any one. 10 Then Simon Peter, having a sword, drew it and struck the servant of the high priest and cut off his right ear. And the name of thee servant was Malchus. 11 Jesus therefore said to Peter: Put up thy sword into the scabbard. The chalice which my father hath given me, shall I not drink it? 12 Then the band and the tribune and the servants of the Jews took Jesus and bound him. 13 And they led him away to Annas first, for he was father-in-law to Caiphas, who was the high priest of that year. 14 Now Caiphas was he who had given the counsel to the Jews: That it was expedient that one man should die for the people. 15 And Simon Peter followed Jesus: and so did another disciple. And that disciple was known to the high priest and went in with Jesus into the court of the high priest. 16 But Peter stood at the door without. The other disciple therefore, who was known to the high priest, went out and spoke to the portress and brought in Peter. 17 The maid therefore that was portress saith to Peter: Art not thou also one of this man's disciple? He saith I am not. 18 Now the servants and ministers stood at a fire of coals, because it was cold, and warmed themselves. And with them was Peter also, standing and warming himself. 19 The high priest therefore asked Jesus of his disciples and of his doctrine. 20 Jesus answered him: I have spoken openly to the world. I have always taught in the synagogue and in the temple, whither all the Jews resort: and in secret I have spoken nothing. 21 Why askest thou me? Ask them who have heard what I have spoken unto them. Behold they know what things I have said. 22 And when he had said these things, one of the servants standing by gave Jesus a blow, saying: Answerest thou the high priest so? 23 Jesus answered him: If I have spoken evil, give testimony of the evil; but if well, why strikest thou me? 24 And Annas sent him bound to Caiphas the high priest. 25 And Simon Peter was standing and warming himself. They said therefore to him: Art not thou also one of his disciples? He denied it and said: I am not. 26 One of the servants of the high priest (a kinsman to him whose ear Peter cut off) saith to him: Did not I see thee in the garden with him? 27 Again therefore Peter denied: and immediately the cock crew. 28 Then they led Jesus from Caiphas to the governor's hall. And it was morning: and they went not into the hall, that they might not be defiled, but that they might eat the pasch. 29 Pilate therefore went out to them, and said: What accusation bring you against this man? 30 They answered and said to him: If he were not a malefactor, we would not have delivered him up to thee. 31 Pilate therefore said to them: Take him you, and judge him according to your law. The Jews therefore said to him: It is not lawful for us to put any man to death. 32 That the word of Jesus might be fulfilled, which he said, signifying what death he should die. 33 Pilate therefore went into the hall again and called Jesus and said to him: Art thou the king of the Jews? 34 Jesus answered: Sayest thou this thing of thyself, or have others told it thee of me? 35 Pilate answered: Am I a Jew? Thy own nation and the chief priests have delivered thee up to me. What hast thou done? 36 Jesus answered: My kingdom is not of this world. If my kingdom were of this world, my servants would certainly strive that I should not be delivered to the Jews: but now my kingdom is not from hence. 37 Pilate therefore said to him: Art thou a king then? Jesus answered: Thou sayest that I am a king. For this was I born, and for this came I into the world; that I should give testimony to the truth. Every one that is of the truth heareth my voice. 38 Pilate saith to him: What is truth? And when he said this, he went out again to the Jews and saith to them: I find no cause in him. 39 But you have a custom that I should release one unto you at the Pasch. Will you, therefore, that I release unto you the king of the Jews? 40 Then cried they all again, saying: Not this man, but Barabbas. Now Barabbas was a robber.

JOHN CHAPTER 19

The continuation of the history of
the Passion of Christ.

1 Then therefore Pilate took Jesus and scourged him. 2 And the soldiers platting a crown of thorns, put it upon his head:and they put on him a purple garment. 3 And they came to him and said: Hail, king of the Jews. And they gave him blows. 4 Pilate therefore went forth again and saith to them: Behold, I bring him forth unto you, that you may know that I find no cause in him. 5 (Jesus therefore came forth, bearing the crown of thorns and the purple garment.) And he saith to them: Behold the Man. 6 When the chief priests, therefore, and the servants had seen him, they cried out, saying: Crucify him, Crucify him. Pilate saith to them: Take him you, and crucify him: for I find no cause in him. 7 The Jews answered him: We have a law; and according to the law he ought to die, because he made himself the Son of God. 8 When Pilate therefore had heard this saying, he feared the more. 9 And he entered into the hall again; and he said to Jesus: Whence art thou? But Jesus gave him no answer. 10 Pilate therefore saith to him: Speakest thou not to me? Knowest thou not that I have power to crucify thee, and I have power to release thee? 11 Jesus answered: Thou shouldst not have any power against me, unless it were given thee from above. Therefore, he that hath delivered me to thee hath the greater sin. 12 And from henceforth Pilate sought to release him. But the Jews cried out, saying: If thou release this man, thou art not Caesar's friend. For whosoever maketh himself a king

speaketh against Caesar. 13 Now when Pilate had heard these words, he brought Jesus forth and sat down in the judgment seat, in the place that is called Lithostrotos, and in Hebrew Gabbatha. 14 And it was the parasceve of the pasch, about the sixth hour: and he saith to the Jews: Behold your king.[27] 15 But they cried out: Away with him: Away with him: Crucify him. Pilate saith to them: shall I crucify your king? The chief priests answered: We have no king but Caesar. 16 Then therefore he delivered him to them to be crucified. And they took Jesus and led him forth. 17 And bearing his own cross, he went forth to the place which is called Calvary, but in Hebrew Golgotha. 18 Where they crucified him, and with him two others, one on each side, and Jesus in the midst. 19 And Pilate wrote a title also: and he put it upon the cross. And the writing was: JESUS OF NAZARETH, THE KING OF THE JEWS. 20 This title therefore many of the Jews did read: because the place where Jesus was crucified was nigh to the city. And it was written in Hebrew, in Greek, and in Latin. 21 Then the chief priests of the Jews said to Pilate: Write not: The King of the Jews. But that he said: I am the King of the Jews. 22 Pilate answered: What I have written, I have written. 23 The soldiers therefore, when they had crucified him, took his garments, (and they made four

---

27 The parasceve of the pasch... That is, the day before the paschal sabbath. The eve of every sabbath was called the parasceve, or day of preparation. But this was the eve of a high sabbath, viz., that which fell in the paschal week.

parts, to every soldier a part) and also his coat. Now the coat was without seam, woven from the top throughout. 24 They said then one to another: Let us not cut it but let us cast lots for it, whose it shall be; that the scripture might be fulfilled, saying: They have parted my garments among them, and upon my vesture they have cast lots. And the soldiers indeed did these things. 25 Now there stood by the cross of Jesus, his mother and his mother's sister, Mary of Cleophas, and Mary Magdalen. 26 When Jesus therefore had seen his mother and the disciple standing whom he loved, he saith to his mother: Woman, behold thy son. 27 After that, he saith to the disciple: Behold thy mother. And from that hour, the disciple took her to his own. 28 Afterwards, Jesus knowing that all things were now accomplished, that the scripture might be fulfilled, said: I thirst. 29 Now there was a vessel set there, full of vinegar. And they, putting a sponge full of vinegar about hyssop, put it to his mouth. 30 Jesus therefore, when he had taken the vinegar, said: It is consummated. And bowing his head, he gave up the ghost. 31 Then the Jews (because it was the parasceve), that the bodies might not remain upon the cross on the sabbath day (for that was a great sabbath day), besought Pilate that their legs might be broken: and that they might be taken away. 32 The soldiers therefore came: and they broke the legs of the first, and of the other that was crucified with him. 33 But after they were come to Jesus, when they saw that he was already dead, they did not break his legs. 34 But one of the soldiers with a spear opened his side: and immediately there came out blood and water. 35 And he that saw it hath given testimony: and his testimony is true. And he knoweth that he saith true: that you also may believe. 36 For these things were done that the scripture might be fulfilled: You shall not break a bone of him. 37 And again another scripture saith: They shall look on him whom they pierced. 38 And after these things, Joseph of Arimathea (because he was a disciple of Jesus, but secretly for fear of the Jews), besought Pilate that he might take away the body of Jesus. And Pilate gave leave. He came therefore and took away the body of Jesus. 39 And Nicodemus also came (he who at the first came to Jesus by night), bringing a mixture of myrrh and aloes, about an hundred pound weight. 40 They took therefore the body of Jesus and bound it in linen cloths, with the spices, as the manner of the Jews is to bury. 41 Now there was in the place where he was crucified a garden: and in the garden a new sepulchre, wherein no man yet had been laid. 42 There, therefore, because of the parasceve of the Jews, they laid Jesus: because the sepulchre was nigh at hand.

JOHN CHAPTER 20

Christ's resurrection and manifestation to his disciples.

1 And on the first day of the week, Mary Magdalen cometh early, when it was yet dark, unto the sepulchre: and she saw the stone taken away from the

sepulchre. 2 She ran therefore and cometh to Simon Peter and to the other disciple whom Jesus loved and saith to them: They have taken away the Lord out of the sepulchre: and we know not where they have laid him. 3 Peter therefore went out, and the other disciple: and they came to the sepulchre. 4 And they both ran together: and that other disciple did outrun Peter and came first to the sepulchre. 5 And when he stooped down, he saw the linen cloths lying: but yet he went not in. 6 Then cometh Simon Peter, following him, and went into the sepulchre: and saw the linen cloths lying, 7 And the napkin that had been about his head, not lying with the linen cloths, but apart, wrapped up into one place. 8 Then that other disciple also went in, who came first to the sepulchre: and he saw and believed. 9 For as yet they knew not the scripture, that he must rise again from the dead. 10 The disciples therefore departed again to their home. 11 But Mary stood at the sepulchre without, weeping. Now as she was weeping, she stooped down and looked into the sepulchre, 12 And she saw two angels in white, sitting, one at the head, and one at the feet, where the body of Jesus had been laid. 13 They say to her: Woman, why weepest thou? She saith to them: Because they have taken away my Lord: and I know not where they have laid him. 14 When she had thus said, she turned herself back and saw Jesus standing: and she knew not that it was Jesus. 15 Jesus saith to her: Woman, why weepest thou? Whom seekest thou? She, thinking that it was the gardener, saith to him: Sir, if thou hast taken him hence, tell me where thou hast laid him: and I will take him away. 16 Jesus saith to her: Mary. She turning, saith to him: Rabboni (which is to say, Master). 17 Jesus saith to her: Do not touch me: for I am not yet ascended to my Father. But go to my brethren and say to them: I ascend to my Father and to your Father, to my God and to your God. 18 Mary Magdalen cometh and telleth the disciples: I have seen the Lord; and these things he said to me. 19 Now when it was late the same day, the first of the week, and the doors were shut, where the disciples were gathered together, for fear of the Jews, Jesus came and stood in the midst and said to them: Peace be to you.[28] 20 And when he had said this, he shewed them his hands and his side. The disciples therefore were glad, when they saw the Lord. 21 He said therefore to them again: Peace be to you. As the Father hath sent me, I also send you. 22 When he had said this, he breathed on them; and he said to them: Receive ye the Holy Ghost. 23 Whose sins you shall forgive, they are forgiven them: and whose sins you shall retain, they are retained.[29] 24 Now Thomas, one of the twelve, who is called Didymus, was not with them when Jesus

---

28 The doors were shut... The same power which could bring Christ's whole body, entire in all its dimensions, through the doors, can without the least question make the same body really present in the sacrament; though both the one and the other be above our comprehension.

29 Whose sins, etc... See here the commission, stamped by the broad seal of heaven, by virtue of which the pastors of Christ's church absolve

came. 25 The other disciples therefore said to him: We have seen the Lord. But he said to them: Except I shall see in his hands the print of the nails and put my finger into the place of the nails and put my hand into his side, I will not believe. 26 And after eight days, again his disciples were within, and Thomas with them. Jesus cometh, the doors being shut, and stood in the midst and said: Peace be to you. 27 Then he said to Thomas: Put in thy finger hither and see my hands. And bring hither the hand and put it into my side. And be not faithless, but believing. 28 Thomas answered and said to him: My Lord and my God. 29 Jesus saith to him: Because thou hast seen me, Thomas, thou hast believed: blessed are they that have not seen and have believed. 30 Many other signs also did Jesus in the sight of his disciples, which are not written in this book. 31 But these are written, that you may believe that Jesus is the Christ, the Son of God: and that believing, you may have life in his name.

JOHN CHAPTER 21

Christ manifests himself to his disciples by the sea side and gives Peter the charge of his sheep.

1 After this, Jesus shewed himself to the disciples at the sea of Tiberias. And he shewed himself after this manner. 2 There were together: Simon Peter and Thomas, who is called Didymus, and Nathanael, who

---

repenting sinners upon their confession.

was of Cana of Galilee, and the sons of Zebedee and two others of his disciples. 3 Simon Peter saith to them: I go a fishing. They say to him: We also come with thee. And they went forth and entered into the ship: and that night they caught nothing. 4 But when the morning was come, Jesus stood on the shore: yet the disciples knew not that it was Jesus. 5 Jesus therefore said to them: Children, have you any meat? They answered him: No. 6 He saith to them: Cast the net on the right side of the ship; and you shall find. They cast therefore: and now they were not able to draw it, for the multitude of fishes. 7 That disciple therefore whom Jesus loved said to Peter: It is the Lord. Simon Peter, when he heard that it was the Lord, girt his coat about him (for he was naked) and cast himself into the sea. 8 But the other disciples came in the ship (for they were not far from the land, but as it were two hundred cubits) dragging the net with fishes. 9 As soon then as they came to land they saw hot coals lying, and a fish laid thereon, and bread. 10 Jesus saith to them: Bring hither of the fishes which you have now caught. 11 Simon Peter went up and drew the net to land, full of great fishes, one hundred and fifty-three. And although there were so many, the net was not broken. 12 Jesus saith to them: Come and dine. And none of them who were at meat, durst ask him: Who art thou? Knowing that it was the Lord. 13 And Jesus cometh and taketh bread and giveth them: and fish in like manner. 14 This is now the third time that Jesus was manifested to his disciples, after he was risen from the dead. 15 When therefore they had dined, Jesus saith to Simon Peter: Simon, son of John, lovest thou me more than these? He saith to him: Yea, Lord, thou knowest that I love thee. He saith to him: Feed my lambs. 16 He saith to him again: Simon, son of John, lovest thou me? He saith to him: yea, Lord, thou knowest that I love thee. He saith to him: Feed my lambs. 17 He said to him the third time: Simon, son of John, lovest thou me? Peter was grieved because he had said to him the third time: Lovest thou me? And he said to him: Lord, thou knowest all things: thou knowest that I love thee. He said to him: Feed my sheep.[30] 18 Amen, amen, I say to thee, When thou wast younger, thou didst gird thyself and didst walk where thou wouldst. But when thou shalt be old, thou shalt stretch forth thy hands, and another shall gird thee and lead thee whither thou wouldst not. 19 And this he said, signifying by what death he should glorify God. And when he had said this, he saith to him: Follow me. 20 Peter turning about, saw that disciple whom Jesus loved following, who also leaned on his breast at supper and said: Lord, who is he that shall betray thee? 21 Him therefore when Peter had seen, he saith to Jesus: Lord, and what shall this man do? 22 Jesus saith to him: So I will have him to remain till I come, what is it to thee? Follow thou me. 23 This

---

30 Feed my sheep... Our Lord had promised the spiritual supremacy to St. Peter; St. Matt. 16. 19; and here he fulfils that promise, by charging him with the superintendency of all his sheep, without exception; and consequently of his whole flock, that is, of his own church.

saying therefore went abroad among the brethren, that that disciple should not die. And Jesus did not say to him: He should not die; but: So I will have him to remain till I come, what is it to thee? 24 This is that disciple who giveth testimony of these things and hath written these things: and we know that his testimony is true. 25 But there are also many other things which Jesus did which, if they were written every one, the world itself. I think, would not be able to contain the books that should be written.

THE END

Printed in Great Britain
by Amazon